With One Heart, With One Voice

Learning to teach and admonish one another in song

by Hal Hammons

ONE STONE
BIBLICAL RESOURCES

Published by:
One Stone Press
979 Lovers Lane
Bowling Green, KY 42103

Printed in the United States of America

ISBN 10: 1941422063
ISBN 13: 978-1-941422-06-9

Supplemental Materials Available:
PowerPoint slides for each lesson
Answer key
Downloadable PDF

ONE STONE
BIBLICAL RESOURCES

www.onestone.com

Preface

My love for singing is well known to anyone who has shared a church pew with me (or a church auditorium, for that matter). So when Andy Alexander approached me with the idea of a workbook dealing with hymns, I was intrigued. Quickly we developed the idea for a book that would combine hymn history, musical training, Biblical instruction and personal motivation—all through the use of spiritual songs. I hope you find it useful.

With One Heart, With One Voice was written with the idea of it being used in church Bible class settings, with enough lessons for two 12-week quarters. You may find it suitable for small, private sessions, a jumping-off point for more in-depth study, or just personal enrichment. The goal is to help us appreciate the importance of song worship, provide correction where necessary, and stimulate personal examination—in short, "with all wisdom teaching one another in psalms, hymns and spiritual songs" (Colossians 3:16).

A few points of order:

Hymn stories are only as accurate as the storytellers and their memories. Especially with regard to hymns 200-300 years old, or even older, the stories become less and less authoritative. The internet, that wonderfully accessible and woefully unreliable source of information, is the source for virtually all of the stories from previous centuries in this book. As the saying goes, it is what it is. Some stories vary, sometimes widely, in the telling. I have tried to provide a reasonable summation of the histories, giving preference to the versions that seemed most reasonable. Complete accuracy is not assured, and in fact is probably not attainable at all. If you are interested in the stories behind the hymns, tremendous work online and in print has been done by people who had far better access and far more time than I; please seek them out. And if I have garbled or mangled any of them, particularly with regard to recent hymns, my deepest apologies; please get in touch, and I will try to make corrections in future editions.

Different groups will likely want to use this book in different ways. Some may find the musical instruction entirely superfluous and boring, either because they care nothing for the technical aspects of music or they are too advanced to benefit from the rudimentary instruction I provide here. Some may not feel it is appropriate to tell in church settings stories about people who do not appear in the Bible. Some may want to spend the entire session singing. That's fine. My goal was to have something for everybody—enough material and questions for two 45-minute sessions per half-lesson, with the idea that most groups will whittle that down by half.

I am fully aware that this book features and lauds hymn writers who do not or did not hold to the same doctrine, or even the same form of worship, that I do. I have no ethical or doctrinal problem with that whatsoever. These men and women's work has enhanced my life ever since I exited the womb, and by the grace of God will continue to do so for the rest of my days. I owe them a debt. We all do. God will be the judge of us all.

Special thanks go to Andy and his crew at One Stone, who do the best work in the business as far as one humble writer is concerned. Also Tim Berman, who did our hymn typesetting, gets kudos for his great work. Tim, who may be the only man on the planet who loves church music more than me, did tremendous work at slave's wages, asking only that we plug the terrific work he does distributing hymns through songsofthechurch.org. And Jerry Tesch deserves special accolades for the song recordings of the hymns that are being produced in conjunction with this book—both for his amazing talent and work and for his willingness to deal with an intrusive writer who kept clogging up his inbox. If you haven't heard him and his Narrow Way colleagues sing, you are the worse for it.

To Glenda Schales (whose hymn supplies the title for this book), Charli Couchman, Matt Bassford, Tim Stevens, Gerald McBride, Kelly and Jo Hersey, Richard Morrison, Craig Roberts, Jay Conner, Ken Young, Robert Taylor, Melea Jennings, Brian Rainwater, Tim Jennings, Bernice and Sam Landrum, Cliff Rhodes, and everyone else I pestered over the last few months; for permissions granted, stories told, corrections offered and encouragement given—many, many thanks.

Out of respect to the authors and their publishers, and to keep my promise to them, I emphasize—this is not a hymnal, nor is it a resource for hymns to be pilfered. Please go through proper channels to acquire permission to use the work of others; most of them (certainly this one) are thrilled to be asked and glad to comply, often at no cost. But please do not trade on their generosity. Unauthorized copying is theft. Theft is a sin.

Finally, my brethren:

Sing on, ye joyful pilgrims.
Praise Him, praise Him.
Saints, lift your voices.
Revive us again.
God bless you, go with God.
Take the name of Jesus with you.

Hal Hammons
Pace, Florida
May 2014

Table of Contents

For R.J.—

I can hear you singing from here.

Lesson 1

Teach Us How to
REJOICE

Do not be grieved, for the joy of the Lord is your strength.
Nehemiah 8:10

Who do you think of
when you think of joy?

**Whose face
do you see?**

Our typical approach to joy is situational. That is to say, we are perfectly willing and eager to rejoice when life gives us an opportunity to do so—more money, better relationships, or even a spiritual success such as the baptism of a good friend or a learning experience in Bible study. The problem with the situational approach, though, is that it leaves us without joy while we wait for our situation to change. Worse yet, it makes us largely if not mostly subject to the actions of others; if they don't behave the way we want them to behave, they essentially rob us of our joy.

Jesus' approach is different. In the Beatitudes (Matthew 5:3-12), He tells us the "blessed" or approved life is the one characterized by godly activity, not pleasant activity. It even includes decidedly unpleasant activity, such as being persecuted for your faith. The person of faith can find joy—in fact Jesus requires as much in verse 12—not because his circumstances are better, but because his joy has nothing to do with circumstances. He is making choices in this life so as to store up "treasures in heaven" (Matthew 6:20), just like countless others have done in times past and continue to do today.

The wonderful thing about rejoicing in the Lord is, first, that you can do it anywhere, anytime. You do not have to wait for a pay raise; you do not have to be married or have children; you just have to walk in faith. And secondly, the behavior of others becomes entirely irrelevant. If problems with family members, neighbors, or even the state of the world persist or increase, that only provides that much more incentive to think more about heavenly things.

Who is your person of joy? Describe the impact his or her attitude has on you and others._____

_____

Share a situation in which you were able to find joy despite adverse circumstances. _____

_____

_____

About the hymn

Ludwig von Beethoven's use of voices in the final movement of his Ninth Symphony was unprecedented. He adapted a poem written in 1785 by Friedrich Schiller that emphasized the joy of life that testifies to a loving Creator. The famous "Ode to Joy," perhaps the most familiar piece of music in his entire catalog, was the result.

A partial translation from the original German of the Schiller poem follows:

> *Joy, beautiful spark of the divinity,*
> *Daughter from Elysium,*
> *We enter your sanctuary, burning with fervor,*
> *O heavenly being!*
>
> *Your magic brings together*
> *what custom has sternly divided.*
> *All men shall become brothers,*
> *wherever your gentle wings hover.*
>
> *Gladly, just as His suns hurtle*
> *through the glorious universe,*
> *So you, brothers, should run your course,*
> *joyfully, like a conquering hero.*

Beethoven was completely deaf as he directed the orchestra and chorus when the symphony premiered in 1824. Focused on the score, he did not realize he was still conducting after the symphony had been completed. A soloist came to the lectern and turned him to face the audience; though he could not hear their applause, he was able to see the raised hands, thrown hats and handkerchiefs, and other demonstrations of the crowd's enthusiastic approval. Beethoven also composed the music for "How Shall the Young Secure Their Hearts?"

LUDWIG VON BEETHOVEN

Edward Hodges arranged "Ode to Joy" for congregational use in 1864. Born in Bristol, England, in 1796, he emigrated and had a long career as an organist and musical director in Canada and the United States; he was the first organist of New York City's famous Trinity Church when it was begun in 1846, playing an organ built to his own specifications. He retired to England and died there in 1867. He is credited with at least four hymn compositions but none so popular as his "Ode to Joy" arrangement.

Numerous texts have been paired with Hodges' arrangement for use in churches; perhaps the most familiar is Henry Van Dyke's "Joyful, Joyful, We Adore Thee." In 1907 Van Dyke was guided by Schiller's poem to write words in English to accompany

Joyful, Joyful, We Adore Thee

1. Joy - ful, joy - ful, we a - dore Thee, God of glo - ry, Lord of love;
2. All Thy works with joy sur - round Thee; Earth and heav'n re - flect Thy rays;
3. Thou art giv - ing and for - giv - ing, Ev - er bless - ing, ev - er blessed,
4. Mor - tals join the might - y cho - rus, Which the morn - ing stars be - gan;

Hearts un - fold like flow'rs be - fore Thee, Op - 'ning to the sun a - bove.
Stars and an - gels sing a - round Thee, Cen - ter of un - bro - ken praise,
Well - spring of the joy of liv - ing, O - cean depth of hap - py rest!
Fa - ther love is reign - ing o'er us; Broth - er love binds man to man.

Melt the clouds of sin and sad - ness; Drive the dark of doubt a - way;
Field and for - est, vale and moun - tain, Flow - 'ry mead - ow, flash - ing sea,
Thou our Fa - ther, Christ our Broth - er, All who live in love are Thine.
Ev - er sing - ing, march we on - ward, Vic - tors in the midst of strife.

Giv - er of im - mor - tal glad - ness, Fill us with the light of day!
Chant - ing bird and flow - ing foun - tain Call us to re - joice in Thee.
Teach us how to love each oth - er; Lift us to the joy di - vine.
Joy - ful mu - sic leads us sun - ward In the tri - umph song of life.

Words: Henry Van Dyke
Music: "Hymn to Joy," Ludwig van Beethoven, arr. Edward Hodges

G - 4 - MI

Beethoven's music. He wrote of his work, "These verses are simple expressions of common Christian feelings and desires in this present time—hymns of today that may be sung together by people who know the thought of the age, and are not afraid that any truth of science will destroy religion, or any revolution on earth overthrow the kingdom of heaven. Therefore this is a hymn of trust and joy and hope."

HENRY VAN DYKE

What do you like or not like about this hymn? _____

_____

_____

_____

Share with the class another older hymn that has a similar theme. Do you think this hymn does a better or worse job of teaching us about rejoicing than "Joyful, Joyful We Adore Thee"? Explain your answer. _____

_____

_____

_____

About the lyrics

Hearts unfold like flowers before Thee,
Opening to the sun above.

Many flowers, such as morning glories, are known for opening their blooms during the day to allow the sunshine in. The sun, an obvious image connoting life, warmth and illumination, is often used as a symbol for God, particularly in pagan lore but also in the Bible—"For the Lord God is a sun and shield; the Lord gives grace and glory; no good thing does He withhold from those who walk uprightly" (Psalm 84:11; see also Isaiah 60:19-20, Revelation 22:5, etc.).

The image of a heart opening itself up to the glory of God and drinking in the blessings He provides daily brings to mind 2 Corinthians 4:6—"For God, who said, 'Light shall shine out of darkness,' is the One who has shone in our hearts to give the Light of the knowledge of the glory of God in the face of Christ." As it is natural for a flower to embrace the sunshine, so also it should be natural for the child of God to open his heart to receive the blessings from above, and then open his mouth to express his gratitude for them and his praise for their Giver.

Name another song that uses imagery from nature to praise God. Why are such images so attractive to songwriters and singers?_____

_____

_____

Supply a line of verse to accompany this one. Try to make the lines have the same number of syllables and have emphasis in the same places. Rhymes need not be exact but should at least be close. Feel free to rework the line that is supplied to fit your own line.

"My life is filled with joy and song . . ."

_____

About the music: time signature

The two numbers on the left of each line of music, to the right of the treble or bass clef, constitute the time signature. It is to be read as a fraction. The top number of the fraction designates how many beats will be in a measure; the bottom number in the fraction designates what note will count as a beat.

4/4 time, as in "Joyful, Joyful, We Adore Thee," is the most frequently used time signature in spiritual music, and probably in music as a whole; it is often called "common time." In the time signature, the bottom number is a 4, so the beat will be given with quarter notes. (Like with an ordinary fraction, a 4 at the bottom stands for a quarter just as a 2 would stand for a half or an 8 for an eighth.) The top number is also a 4, indicating there are four beats per measure.

Most of the notes in "Joyful, Joyful We Adore Thee" are quarter notes, making it easy to mark the time. A quarter note will have filled-in shapes, unlike the empty half notes you see at the end of each line of this song. A typical measure of the song, then, will have four quarter notes. But regardless of how many notes appear on the page, each measure gets four full beats.

Find another older song in 4/4 time and beat time to the words of that song as you recite the words aloud with the group. _____

_____

Lesson 1A

Teach Us How to
REJOICE EVEN MORE

Rejoice in the Lord always; again I will say, rejoice!
Philippians 4:4

What can I do to have Biblical joy in my life?

Why isn't this me?

The book of Philippians is all about rejoicing. Paul refused to allow his attitude to be defined by his situation in life— even in a prison cell. Yes, he seems to have anticipated a release from prison in relatively short order, but he wasn't going to wait until then to live in joy. And his letter encourages his readers, and us as well, to find joy in challenging places as well. And if our rejoicing is "in the Lord" (Philippians 3:1, 4:4), we should have little trouble finding it.

The problem is, we (like our friends in the sinful world around us) tend to want to find joy in our immediate surroundings. As a result, we are constantly altering our surroundings to maximize our pleasure in the short term. Better friends. A bigger house. More money— always more money. We are eager to experience joy when the things of this life go our way. But we cannot find it in times of hardship. In fact, we often will absolutely refuse to find joy; depression, anxiety and want serve as motivations for us to "improve" our lives.

Christians have ample opportunity for joy in this life, and we absolutely should pursue it—and, finding it, glorify God for His manifold grace and love. But if our ultimate reward is not of this earth, neither should be our ultimate joy. Joy based on our relationship with God, which cannot be shaken by circumstances (Romans 8:38-39), serves as an emotional buffer during times of emotional extremes. It buoys our spirits in times of hardship to know our work in His service, even when it brings us pain, "is not in vain in the Lord" (1 Corinthians 15:58). But it also grounds us when we are tempted to think too highly of ourselves; even when Satan falls at our feet, Jesus says, "Nevertheless do not rejoice in this . . . but rejoice that your names are recorded in heaven" (Luke 10:20).

What is keeping you from rejoicing? Share with the class if you are comfortable doing so. _____

_____

Share an example, perhaps from your own experience, of how short-term joy and long-term joy can come in conflict. _____

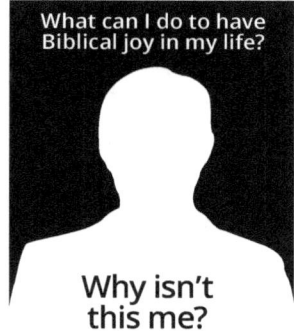

_____

_____

Now My Spirit Soars

1. There were times in my life when I searched thru my soul
2. When I o - pened my eyes, let my heart see the way

And longed for the mean - ing of life;
That leads to the heav - ens a - bove;

Need - ed strength and re - lease from my bur - den of cares,
Then my hun - ger was filled and my thirst-ing was quenched,

Re - lease from all my wor - ry and my strife.
I breathed new life as I o - beyed His will.

CHORUS

Now my spir - it soars as high as an ea - gle in the sky; (My)

My Lord re - stored the hope in my soul. (my soul.)

I see in His Word all I need in my life;

The pow - er of His grace that makes me whole.

Words: Melea Jennings
Music: Melea Jennings, arr. Brian Rainwater
© 2002 Melea Jennings

E♭ - 4 - DO

About the hymn

MELEA JENNINGS

Melea Jennings is a Christian in Lakeland, Florida. She claims no special musical training, only a lifetime of singing with the saints. She has written several songs that have been widely circulated among brethren, including "Thank You, Lord."

Melea's son, Jesse, was a young man going through the trials common to young men. The choices and pressures that weighed on him weighed on his mother as well. Melea remembers going into her closet, literally, after a heart-wrenching prayer to God for her son, and coming out with the lyrics to the first verse. She called her mother to share her work and get her feedback; her mother's advice: "OK, now 'take it up' from there!" Encouraged, Melea made a point of making the chorus and second verse especially inspiring and uplifting, showing the impact an attitude of faith can have on the one who is struggling with his or her situation in life.

BRIAN RAINWATER

Brian Rainwater, a friend of Melea's, arranged the song. A native of Fort Smith, Arkansas, Brian currently works as the Director of Bands at Florida College in Temple Terrace, Florida. He has written several songs in use among churches, including "Nothing Is Impossible with God" and "Lord God Almighty." One of Brian's students recommended him to Melea after having sung some of Brian's music with the FC chorus.

What do you like or not like about this hymn? _____

_____

_____

Share with the class another newer hymn that has a similar theme. Do you think this hymn does a better or worse job of teaching us about rejoicing than "Now My Spirit Soars"? Explain your answer. _____

_____

_____

About the lyrics

Now my spirit soars as high
As an eagle in the sky.

Eagles have been seen as images of freedom and exaltation probably as long as there have been eagles—likely because they fly so high. People who have looked out windows in airplanes (or better yet, viewed the world below while skydiving or parasailing) have experienced the sensation of seeing the world from on high; the problems and squabbles of the world seem to fade into insignificance with every extra foot of altitude. But even before man could fly, man could imagine what it would be like to soar.

The best known eagle image from the Bible is almost certainly found in Isaiah 40:31— "Yet those who wait for the Lord will gain new strength; they will mount up with wings like eagles, they will run and not get tired, they will walk and not become weary." The power that God supplies for the Christian does not always arrive according to the Christian's timetable, but it does arrive; when it does, he finds the power in ample supply.

List some other passages of Scripture that include images of eagles and/or flight. Describe the impressions that such passages leave with you when you read them. _____

_____

_____

List some songs that include images of eagles and/or flight. Describe the impressions that such songs leave with you when you sing them. _____

_____

_____

About the music: rhythm

Most older hymns have a very strong beat to them—that is, the music naturally emphasizes the syllables in certain parts of the measure, especially the first one. This is why hymn writers use "Jesus" and "God" at the beginning of measures so frequently; words that deserve extra stress naturally receive it.

Many modern hymns are more syncopated. The beat is more difficult to find. In "Now My Spirit Soars," the first and third of the four beats in every measure (the most important ones in 4/4 time, the ones that drive the song rhythmically) are emphasized, but the second and fourth beats often fall between notes. Since so much common music is phrased this way, those who sing "by ear" will likely not have much trouble adjusting; they very well may find this rhythm more interesting to sing. This will only happen, though, if the leader knows the song well, enunciates while leading, and emphasizes the first and third beats.

The word rhythm implies synchronicity, consistent and even flow, and minimal disturbances. Rhythm is a critical element when asking multiple individuals to teach and worship as a single unit. The more complex the song, the more difficult it is to sing in unison. Worship leaders should consider this when choosing syncopated songs for use in the congregation—particularly songs not well known to the group.

Find another song with a complex rhythm. Discuss the rhythm before singing it. Afterward, discuss what part if any such songs should play in congregational worship. _____

_____

A final admonition

Philippians 4:4 is not optional any more than Philippians 2:3, Ephesians 6:1, Colossians 3:17, or any other requirement placed on us by Paul and the other inspired New Testament writers. Paul is not telling us merely how to find the maximum degree of satisfaction and peace in our walk with Christ; he is telling us what Jesus Christ looks like in the heart of a Christian. A failure to find joy in one's life in Christ is not merely a joy problem; fundamentally it is a faith problem—either a failure to believe one's life is blessed and secure when given over to the Lord, or a realization that one's life is not actually given over to the Lord at all.

Find your joy in your faith. Remind yourself constantly how blessed you are in Jesus (Ephesians 1:3). Do not allow your attention to be diverted by the mundane things of this life. The more you dwell on the things "worthy of praise" (Philippians 4:8), the more prepared to praise God you will be.

Lesson 2

Teach Us How to
PRAY

Pray without ceasing.
1 Thessalonians 5:17

Who do you think of when
you think of prayer?

**Whose face
do you see?**

Praying is unnatural. Our instinct is always to act, especially to pursue our own well-being. It takes faith in its purest form to instead ask someone else to act—particularly an unseen God. And that is why prayer is such an integral part of the Christian's life. It shows, more than any other thing he can do, that he trusts God more than he trusts himself. That, of course, assumes the prayer is being offered in faith. Anyone can throw words at the ceiling and hope for a good outcome. Praying and believing that the prayer is heard and acknowledged, believing that it actually makes a difference—that's the tricky part.

Perhaps that is part of the reason prayer is taught to us by the Lord Himself in very simple concept. "Pray, then, in this way," Jesus says in Matthew 6:9-13. Acknowledge and praise your heavenly Father. Accept His lordship. Give thanks for everyday blessings. Forgive our past sins, and guard us against future ones. It doesn't have to be fancy; in fact, it shouldn't be fancy. We're not informing God of the things He needs to know about our lives, after all (Matthew 6:32, 7:11). We are reminding ourselves of the connection we have to God, and of why we need it. It's a faith exercise at its core.

The greatest test of our faith in prayer is when we do not get what we want or expect. We are assured that God hears and answers prayers asked "according to His will" (1 John 5:14-15). This does not mean that God will give us our request if He feels like it; it means He has a will for our lives—being conformed to the image of Jesus (Romans 8:29). That is how we find peace when we pray (Philippians 4:6-7)—we make our requests, and then we say, as He did in the garden, "yet not My will, but Yours be done" (Luke 22:42).

Who is your person of prayer? Describe the impact his or her attitude has on you and others. _____

_____

Share an approach you use to make prayer more effective for you—timing, subject matter, environment, preparation, etc. _____

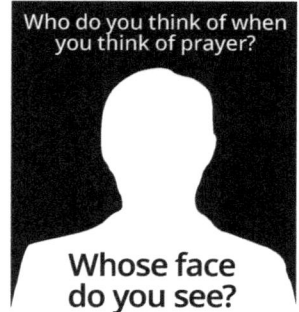

_____

_____

What a Friend We Have in Jesus

1. What a friend we have in Je - sus, All our sins and griefs to bear!
What a friend we have in Je - sus, All our sins and griefs to bear!
2. Have we tri - als and temp - ta - tions? Is there trou - ble an - y - where?
Have we tri - als and temp - ta - tions? Is there trou - ble an - y - where?
3. Are we weak and heav - y - lad - en, Cum - bered with a load of care?
Are we weak and heav - y - lad - en, Cum - bered with a load of care?

What a priv - i - lege to car - ry Eve - ry - thing to God in prayer!
What a priv - i - lege to car - ry Eve - ry - thing to God in prayer!
We should nev - er be dis - cour - aged; Take it to the Lord in prayer.
We should nev - er be dis - cour - aged; Take it to the Lord in prayer.
Pre - cious Sav - ior, still our ref - uge, Take it to the Lord in Prayer.
Pre - cious Sav - ior, still our ref - uge, Take it to the Lord in Prayer.

O what peace we of - ten for - feit, O what need - less pain we bear,
O what peace we of - ten for - feit, O what need - less pain we bear,
Can we find a friend so faith - ful Who will all our sor - rows share?
Can we find a friend so faith - ful Who will all our sor - rows share?
Do your friends de - spise, for - sake you? Take it to the Lord in prayer!
Do your friends de - spise, for - sake you? Take it to the Lord in prayer!

All be - cause we do not car - ry   Eve - ry - thing to God in prayer.
All be - cause we do not car - ry Eve - ry - thing to God in prayer.
Je - sus knows our eve - ry weak - ness;   Take it to the Lord in prayer.
Je - sus knows our eve - ry weak - ness; Take it to the Lord in prayer.
In His arms He'll take and shield you;   You will find a sol - ace there.
In His arms He'll take and shield you; You will find a sol - ace there.

Words: Joseph Medlicott Scriven
Music: "Converse," Charles C. Converse, arr. R. J. Stevens

F - 4 - SOL

About the hymn

JOSEPH M. SCRIVEN

Joseph M. Scriven's life was shrouded in tragedy. Born in 1819 of well-to-do parents in Banbridge, Ireland, and educated at Trinity College, he emigrated to Canada to put distance between himself and his family, from whom he had become estranged because of his faith. Also he was grieving the loss of his fiancée, who had drowned the night before they were to be married. He met another woman in Canada and they were planning to be wed, but she contracted pneumonia suddenly and died. He never married.

Scriven was well known for his attitude of service. When walking down the street dressed in working-man's clothes and carrying a saw horse and saw, a gentleman saw him and inquired after him to perhaps acquire his services. "That is Mr. Scriven," said a neighbor. "He won't cut wood for you." When asked why such was the case, he was told, "Because you are able to pay for it. He only saws wood for poor widows and sick people."

In 1855 he heard word that his mother was sick back in Ireland. He wrote a poem intended to give her comfort, which he entitled, "Pray Without Ceasing." Later it was set to music by Charles Crozat Converse and ultimately became one of the most beloved hymns ever written.

IRA SANKEY

Scriven battled depression late in life. A friend tells the story of having left him at midnight, only to return later and find him missing. His body was discovered in a nearby body of water. Whether his death was intentional or accidental remains unclear.

Ira D. Sankey is credited for bringing "What a Friend We Have in Jesus" to the public's attention. It was the final hymn included in *Sankey's Gospel Hymns Number 1*, one of the first great hymnals in America—"Thus the last hymn that went into the book became one of the first in favor," Sankey said of this hymn.

What do you like or not like about this hymn? _____
_____
_____

Share with the class another older hymn that has a similar theme. Do you think this hymn does a better or worse job of teaching us about prayer than "What a Friend We Have in Jesus"? Explain your answer. _____
_____
_____
_____

About the lyrics

Can we find a friend so faithful,
Who will all our sorrows share?
Jesus knows our ev'ry weakness;
Take it to the Lord in prayer.

Do we pray to Jesus, or *through* Jesus? Is there a significant difference? The debate has raged for centuries. Many of our songs specifically mention praying to Jesus. "What a Friend We Have in Jesus" is not as obvious, but it is still evident for one who examines the lyrics. "The Lord" typically refers to Jesus in the New Testament, although there are exceptions. Jesus is the "friend" to whom we are encouraged to bring our sins and griefs throughout the hymn. Clearly Joseph Scriven considered taking one's prayers "to God" and "to the Lord" interchangeable concepts. The question is, was he right?

All spiritual activity is to be done "in the name of" (or by the authority of) Jesus (Colossians 3:17)—including prayer (John 14:13). As our Intercessor, the Son enables us to draw near to the Father (Hebrews 7:25, Romans 8:34). So any prayer taken to God can be said to have been taken to Jesus also.

The nature of the Godhead is beyond true human understanding. But if Jesus' claim, even on earth, to be one with the Father (John 10:30) means anything, it would seem to mean their actions, motivations and values are intertwined. It would seem unreasonable to make absolute statements about which aspect of the Divine Nature must and must not be addressed in prayer.

What are some other older hymns that seem to endorse praying to Jesus? Are you comfortable singing these hymns? Why or why not? _____

_____

_____

_____

About the music: accidentals and key signature

Flats (♭), sharps (♯) and naturals (♮) are all accidentals. They refer to the way a song writer will alter a note in the music by a half-step. A flat makes a note a half-step lower; a sharp makes it a half-step higher; a natural cancels out a flat or a sharp that occurs either in the same measure or in the key signature.

The key signature is the collection of flats and sharps between the treble or bass clef and the time signature. The key of C has no sharps or flats. That means you could play eight notes on a piano, starting with the C and proceeding up or down, and hit only white keys to make a normal scale. "What A Friend We Have In Jesus" is in the key of

F (shown by the use of a single flat, on the line for B, in the key signature); therefore, unless otherwise notated, every B found in the music is flatted and all other notes retain their normal value.

In R.J. Stevens' arrangement of "What a Friend We Have in Jesus," the B♭ in the tenor line, fourth measure, is given a natural. Then the next note gets a flat, canceling the natural and restoring the B♭ to its original value. Later, in the ninth measure, the soprano has an F♯ and the alto a D♯. That means they only drop a half-step to reach those notes instead of the normal full step from, respectively, a G and an E. The altos have a natural on the F♯ they sing two notes later, canceling the sharp.

Find other older hymns that feature accidentals prominently, especially in the melody. Go through the music in unison to emphasize the effect of accidentals. _____

_____

_____

Lesson 2A

Teach Us How to
PRAY EVEN MORE

Humble yourselves in the presence of the Lord,
and He will exalt you.
James 4:10

> What can I do to have
> Biblical prayer in my life?
>
> **Why isn't**
> **this me?**

Praying is often seen as a measure of last resort for people who have little or no relationship with God. After having exhausted every conceivable option, when nothing else is left to do, then and only then will they turn to prayer. Unfortunately, often the people of God are not much better. We may be quick to offer prayers at specific times such as meals, worship, and the end of the day. But in times of peril, decision, and stress, often it is still our instinct to take care of circumstances on our own first, and resort to prayer afterword (if at all).

Paul tells us in Philippians 4:6-7, "Be anxious for nothing, but in everything by prayer and supplication with thanksgiving let your requests be made known to God. And the peace of God, which surpasses all comprehension, will guard you hearts and your minds in Christ Jesus." Any opportunity for worry is an opportunity for prayer—or perhaps we should say an *excuse* for prayer. The child of God should always be looking for an opportunity to approach his heavenly Father, whether it be a favorable situation or an unfavorable one.

Prayers need not be lengthy or detailed; Nehemiah's prayer when standing before King Artaxerxes appears to have been accomplished in hardly any time at all (Nehemiah 2:4). They need not even be articulate; when living according to the Spirit can produce nothing more than "groanings too deep for words," these prayers, too, reach God's throne (Romans 8:26-27). After all, "your Father knows what you need before you ask Him" (Matthew 6:8). Shortness or failure of words will not stop a loving Father from listening to His children.

What is keeping you from praying? Share with the class if you are comfortable doing so._____

_____

_____

What are some opportunities for prayer of which we may rob ourselves?

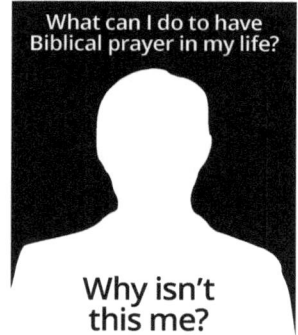

_____

_____

_____

About the hymn

Ken Young is one of the most popular hymn writers and musicians among churches of Christ today. He is the founder and director of Hallal Ministries. Since 1989, Hallal has produced more than 20 albums of acapella music. Young has written numerous songs in common usage in newer hymnals and supplements, including "Faithful Love," "My Eyes Have Seen Your Glory," "Thomas' Song" and "Richly Blest."

KEN YOUNG

Young currently works also as the senior worship minister for the Golf Course Road church of Christ in Midland, Texas.

What do you like or not like about this hymn? _____
_____
_____

Share with the class another newer hymn that has a similar theme. Do you think this hymn does a better or worse job of teaching us about rejoicing than "Constant Prayer"? Explain your answer. _____
_____
_____
_____

About the lyrics

For Your mercy and Your goodness
Are so vast, beyond compare.
To be more like You is still
Our constant prayer.

Part of Paul's characterization of regular Christian activity in Romans 12:12 is "devoted to prayer" ("be constant in prayer" in the English Standard Version). Since being more like Christ ("conformed to the image of [Jesus]" in Romans 8:29) is the central principle of the Christian life, we must always be striving toward it. As Paul writes in Philippians 3:12, "Not that I have already attained it or have already become perfect but I press on so that I may lay hold of that for which also I was laid hold of by Christ Jesus." Since we have not yet attained it either, we also must press forward. Prayer helps us do just that.

We generally see Bible study as the tool by which personal growth is accomplished, and it is. But prayer is a powerful partner for study. When our best efforts are paired with prayer to God for wisdom to use the answers we find in His word (James 1:5-8), as well as prayers for His mercy and patience while we continue to fall short, we find

Constant Prayer

1. Lord, You have giv-en us more than we de-serve.
2. Lord, You're our deep de-sire, our ev-er-last-ing love.
3. Lord, Your a-maz-ing glo-ry pales the bright-est star.

May we nev-er boast in wealth, just teach us how to serve.
Here we are, please seal our hearts for Thy courts a-bove.
No one who is pre-sent here, should won-der where You are.

Help our hearts be o-ver-flow-ing with a will-ing-ness to share.
Use our hands to heal the wound-ed, who just need some-one to care.
For Your mer-cy and Your good-ness are so vast, be-yond com-pare.

To be more like You is still our con-stant prayer.

Words: Ken Young
Music: Ken Young
© 1999 Hallal Music

G - 4 - DO

ourselves even more devoted to Him and His path for our lives, more reminded of the perfect Example that is set for us, and more anxious for the day our perfection will be completed by Him in heaven.

How can we phrase our prayers in such a way as to encourage action on our parts, rather than simply waiting for God to act? _____

_____

_____

_____

List some songs that read like prayers. Describe ways we can use these song lyrics to improve our public and private prayers._____

_____

_____

_____

About the music: changing time signatures

Occasionally—perhaps for the sake of variety or to better accommodate the lyrics—composers will change the time signature within a song. Most commonly this occurs when a song transitions from one section to another, such as from the verse to the chorus.

Twice in "Constant Prayer" the time signature changes from 4/4 to 2/4 and then back again to 4/4. That means, simply put, that the two measures designated as being in 2/4 time receive only two beats instead of the four beats found throughout the rest of the song. Note that since only two measures are missing the extra two beats, the measures could have been reconstructed in such a way as to keep the entire song in 4/4 time. Clearly the hymn writer felt strongly that the words share, more and still all deserved the extra emphasis that comes naturally from being at the beginning of a measure.

Song directors who do not have much experience with changing time signatures can become easily confused in these situations, and in turn may confuse the congregation. As always, practice is the best safeguard. Until the director masters the transitions, he may choose to direct the entire song with a two-beat system, as though the entire song were written in 2/4 time and the 4/4 measures were cut in half. This will eliminate the awkward transition and still provide a good pattern for the group to follow.

List some other songs that change time signatures. Does changing time signatures make them difficult to sing or lead?_____

_____

_____

Discuss song leaders' use of hand motions. Does it help or hinder the worship experience? Explain your answer._____

_____

_____

A final admonition

Prayer is work. Hard work. And frankly, most people are not up for that. Going through the motions, bowing their head and mumbling "Amen" at church services, that's one thing. But making an actual prayer list and working your way through it, going through the church directory line by line and finding a way to mention every member's name in prayer, getting used to using a spare moment or two at a traffic light or during a commercial break to briefly reconnect with God, that's quite another.

Do your exercises. Work your prayer muscles. Seek someone to be your "spotter" if you need one. Do not be satisfied with a "something is better than nothing" approach to prayer. You would not be satisfied if that were the approach your children made toward you.

Lesson 3

Teach Us How to
TRUST

In God I have put my trust, I shall not be afraid.
What can man do to me?
Psalm 56:11

Who do you think of when
you think of trust?

Whose face
do you see?

We have all seen the team-building exercise where one person is asked to fall backward into the arms of another. Those who have participated remark how much more difficult it is to be the one who trusts than the one in whom trust is placed. It is instinctive to support someone who requires support; however, it is anything but instinctive to put your welfare wholly in the hands of someone else. And as difficult as it is to trust someone who you barely know from the water cooler, it can be far more difficult to trust a God whom you have never seen at all.

But then, we have seen Him. We see Him through His word. We see Him in the face of His Son (2 Corinthians 4:6). Surely our inability to trust in God is rooted in a weak relationship with Him. And just as surely, increasing our understanding of the nature of God and His role in our lives will produce a greater level of trust in His word as adequate to guide our lives.

Solomon writes in Proverbs 3:5-6, "Trust in the Lord with all your heart and do not lean on your own understanding. In all your ways acknowledge Him, and He will make your paths straight." It reminds us of another popular exercise—one in which a blindfolded person is required to walk through a maze with only the directions of his teammates to guide him. The one who is blind is in no position to pick and choose directions to follow; it is all or nothing. When we fully trust in God we will stop judging His words based on good sense, timeliness and the general opinion and simply follow. After all, the only way we can possibly know the way to where we are headed is by following the One who has shown us the way (John 14:4-6).

Who is your person of trust? Describe the impact his or her attitude has on you and others. _____

_____

When are we least likely to trust in God? What should we do in those circumstances?_____

_____

_____

About the hymn

Louisa M.R. Stead, born in or around 1850, was picnicking with her husband and 4-year-old daughter, Lily, by Long Island Sound. During their time there, they heard the cries of a young boy drowning in the ocean. Mr. Stead rushed to his rescue, but, tragically, he and the boy both perished. Mrs. Stead was left widowed and destitute at the age of 29. But she continued to believe her life was secure in the hand of God, despite her misfortunes. She and Lily eventually became missionaries in South Africa and Rhodesia (now Zimbabwe). Three years later

LOUISA M.R. STEAD

the hardship of the loss of her husband and other hardships in her life moved her to write "Tis So Sweet to Trust In Jesus." Instead of shaking her faith, adversity only moved her to lean on the Lord even more firmly.

She died on January 18, 1917, in Rhodesia, by which time it is said that 5,000 natives had learned to sing and love "Tis So Sweet to Trust in Jesus" in their native tongue.

William J. Kirkpatrick is one of the greatest and most prolific writers of music for hymns of the 19th Century, composing music for such familiar hymns as "Lead Me to Calvary," "We Have an Anchor," and "He Hideth My Soul." "Tis So Sweet to Trust in Jesus" first appeared in his collection, *Songs of Triumph*, in 1882. When he passed away suddenly on September 29, 1921, he was working on a new hymn based on the following passage (author

WILLIAM J. KIRKPATRICK

unknown):

Just as Thou wilt, Lord, this is my cry;
Just as Thou wilt, to live or to die;
I am Thy servant; Thou knowest best,
Just as Thou wilt, Lord, labor or rest.

What do you like or not like about this hymn? _____

_____

_____

Share with the class another older hymn that has a similar theme. Do you think this hymn does a better or worse job of teaching us about trust than "Tis So Sweet to Trust in Jesus"? Explain your answer. _____

_____

_____

_____

'Tis So Sweet to Trust in Jesus

1. 'Tis so sweet to trust in Je - sus, Just to take Him at His word,
2. O how sweet to trust in Je - sus! Just to trust His cleans-ing blood,
3. Yes, 'tis sweet to trust in Je - sus, Just from sin and self to cease,
4. I'm so glad I learned to trust Thee, Pre-cious Je - sus, Sav - ior, Friend;

Just to rest up - on His prom - ise, Just to know, "Thus saith the Lord."
Just in sim - ple faith to plunge me 'Neath the heal - ing, clean-ing flood!
Just from Je - sus sim - ply tak - ing Life and rest, and joy and peace.
And I know that Thou art with me, Wilt be with me to the end.

CHORUS

Je - sus, Je - sus, how I trust Him! How I've proved Him o'er and o'er.

Je - sus, Je - sus, pre-cious Je - sus! O for grace to trust Him more!

Words: Louisa M. R. Stead
Music: "Trust in Jesus," William J. Kirkpatrick

Ab - 4 - MI

About the lyrics

Jesus, Jesus, how I trust Him!
How I've proved Him o'er and o'er.

Jesus is under no obligation to "prove" Himself to us; He has already demonstrated all the mercy and love in the world. If ever one person proved his devotion to another, surely it was when "He humbled Himself by becoming obedient to the point of death, even death on a cross" (Philippians 2:8). We "prove" Jesus in the same way a swordsman would prove a blade, or the way the ungrateful dinner invitee in Luke 14:19 proved, or tried out, his new oxen; we employ Jesus in the task to which He is assigned—"the author and perfecter of faith" (Hebrews 12:2)—and watch Him succeed. And unlike a sword or an ox, He cannot possibly do anything other than succeed.

We do not want to put God to the test (Matthew 4:7) by intentionally thrusting ourselves into a difficult situation in the confidence that He will certainly save us. But we can fearlessly go where He has told us to go without wavering. And when we get to that place in our faith journey when we can fall back into the arms of Jesus with absolute trust that He will bear us up, the feeling of invincibility we read of in Romans 8:38-39 is ours—"For I am convinced that neither death, nor life, nor angels, nor principalities, nor things present, nor things to come, nor powers, nor height, nor depth, nor any other created thing, will be able to separate us from the love of God, which is in Christ Jesus our Lord."

May God continue to grace us with opportunities to "trust Him more"!

How has Jesus been "proved" in your own life? _____

_____

_____

_____

How might we "put God to the test" in our lives, and what would be a better way for us to behave in those circumstances? _____

_____

_____

_____

About the music: tempo

To a certain extent, the tempo, or pace, of a song is at the discretion of the director or singers. As a rule, songs written in a 2/4 time ("march time") should be sung at a brisk march tempo (think "The Stars and Stripes Forever") and songs in 3/4 ("waltz time") smoothly without dragging (think "The Blue Danube Waltz" or "Waltz of the Flowers"). Of course, song writers do not always abide by the "rules" others make for them! The "proper" tempo is not always best.

The one hard and fast rule for pacing a hymn is to not go so quickly as to make it too difficult to sing the words. A close second, serving as a bookend to the first, is to not go so slowly as to cause the song to lose its effectiveness. A song allowed to crawl at a snail's pace can become distracting and even boring. The leader should set a pace that is comfortable to sing and effective in conveying the message, and then stick to it. All things being equal, a quicker pace encourages enthusiasm and energy, and a slower pace encourages contemplation and emotional intensity.

A song like "Tis So Sweet to Trust in Jesus" is exciting and encouraging to sing at a quick pace. Allowed to drag, though, it loses its appeal. A small handful of songs ("No, Not One" and "I Stand Amazed" are examples), because of their lyrics that are both encouraging and contemplative, can be sung either quickly or slowly; leaders should choose a tempo that conveys the emotion and purpose of the song service and the worship service as a whole. Serious alterations to a song, especially one well known by the group, should be announced beforehand.

List some songs that are habitually sung too slowly or too quickly. What effect can a poor tempo have on a worship service?_____

_____

_____

_____

If a song leader in the group is willing, have him lead a song at an unusual tempo that he feels is still effective. Discuss the different impact the song has at the new tempo. _____

_____

_____

Lesson 3A

Teach Us How to
TRUST EVEN MORE

Trust in the LORD with all your heart and do not lean on your own understanding.
Proverbs 3:5

What can I do to have Biblical trust in my life?

Why isn't this me?

It's a crazy world. And it seems to be getting crazier by the day. We believe intellectually, as people of faith, that God is watching over the affairs of men and that He judges men for their deeds, even within time. "For the kingdom is the Lord's and He rules over the nations" (Psalm 22:28). Even so, as problems mount and depravity continues to prevail before our eyes, we sometimes wonder if that control is being exercised properly. And by that, of course, we mean it is not being exercised the way we would were we in charge.

But trusting in God doesn't become an antiquated notion in the face of Satan's triumphs; rather, that is when we need trust the most. Shadrach, Meshach and Abed-nego did not end their walk of faith at the door of the fiery furnace; in a sense, that is when it truly began. Their words of confidence in God and defiance of the most powerful man in the world (Daniel 3:17-18) inspire people of faith even today, more than two dozen centuries later.

Trusting in God will not, in and of itself, cure disease or abolish crime or banish poverty. In fact, it probably will not; Jesus Himself said, "you always have the poor with you" (John 12:8). But Christians do not view a lack of justice or decency in the world as evidence of God's neglect, but rather of the toll sin has taken on the world from the fall until now. Peace doesn't come from watching our questions answered; it comes from knowing that, with God, we don't need them to be answered.

Should unforeseen and unfortunate circumstances produce a lack of confidence in God? Why or why not? _____

_____

_____

What is the impact, for good or bad, of trusting in God in our everyday lives?

_____

_____

_____

I Close My Eyes

1. My prayer Je - ho - vah hear to my en - treat - ing cry;
2. Be - cause I trust in Thee, O, cause Thou me to hear

In faith - ful - ness, give ear, in right - eous - ness re - ply.
Thy lov - ing kind - ness free, when morn - ing doth ap - pear.

No God have I but Thee; Teach me to do Thy will;
Make me to know Thy way where - in my path should be;

Thy spir - it's good; Lead me on e - ven path - way still.
Be - cause my soul each day do I lift up to Thee.

CHORUS

I close my eyes; I see His Ma - jes - ty;

I close my eyes; and feel His love for me.

Words: Clarence Johnson and Jay Conner
Music: Jay Conner
© 2000 Jay Conner

E - 4 - SOL

About the hymn

JAY CONNER

Jay Conner is a song writer and concert pianist. In addition to instrumental recordings of his own compositions of piano music, he has a collection of hymns in print, *Songs from the Heart and Soul*, with a corresponding set of recordings He is a regular contributor to the annual 1,000 Voices event in North Carolina.

"I Close My Eyes" is a hymn particularly close to Conner. He says it is the first one that really acquired wide acceptance, although "Praise the Lord, I'm Coming Home" has appeared in *Hymns for Worship* since the revised edition first appeared. Like many current hymns, it gained popularity among young Christians, who came to consider it one of their favorite devotional songs. Quickly it began appearing in congregational hymn supplements, as well as *Hymns for Worship (Supplement)*.

What do you like or not like about this hymn? _____

_____

_____

Share with the class another newer hymn that has a similar theme. Do you think this hymn does a better or worse job of teaching us about trust than "I Close My Eyes"? Explain your answer. _____

_____

_____

_____

About the lyrics

I close my eyes,
I see His majesty,
I close my eyes
And feel His love for me.

Faith, not vision, is necessary to see an invisible God. Certainly there are evidences to God's existence and nature in the world that surrounds us—a beautiful sunrise, the natural processes of weather, the procession of the planets through the solar system. But all of these are merely the effects of the original Cause. Measuring His greatness merely by its effects in the physical world would be like measuring the greatness of a musician based merely on his album sales or downloads.

Ultimately God is unknown and unknowable to mere mortals. We know only what He has chosen to reveal to us of Himself; the complete scope of the greatness of God does not fit within a human brain. In a very real sense, we see Him best with our eyes closed as we consider the greatest greatness possible, and then try to take it a step even further.

This is the dilemma the psalmists wrestle with when they try to describe God to us. Thankfully, through the Holy Spirit, we have the best offerings possible.

Psalm 18:2-3 is a passage describing the power of God that encourages us in prayer. List two or three other similar passages. _____

_____

_____

_____

List the components of prayer mentioned in the model prayer of Matthew 6:9-13. Which of these components occupy the bulk of our prayers? Which gets the least attention? Should that be the case?_____

_____

_____

_____

Describe how a regular prayer life can help us in our daily lives as Christians, regardless of how God responds to those prayers. _____

_____

_____

_____

About the music: tempo alterations

Hymn writers often alter the regular beat of a song, usually for the purpose of enhancing the mood they are trying to convey, sometimes just to simplify the singing process.

One of the most common tools used by the hymn writer is the fermata—also called a "hold" or a "bird's eye." It signifies a note that should be held indefinitely. The congregation is expected to look to the leader at that point to determine exactly when to resume the regular rhythm of the song. Although it is common to slow the tempo down upon returning from a fermata, it is by no means required. Most of the time, particularly toward the middle of a song, the leader is well advised to resume the original tempo to keep the song from dragging to an increasing degree one stanza after another.

Another common tool is the *ritardando*, generally abbreviated as *ritard.* or *rit.* It denotes a gradual slowing of the tempo. It is particularly common at the end of a stanza; in fact, many groups and leaders, particularly with certain songs, may automatically slow down at the end of a stanza whether such is designated in the music or not. In any case, the normal tempo should be assumed after the slowed passage is completed.

Twice in "I Close My Eyes" Jay Conner also adds breaks in the music, signified by a double slash (//). This denotes a brief stoppage, like an extra beat of rest. It does not indicate a slowing of regular tempo either before or after.

In songs with tempo alterations it becomes even more important that the congregation keep its eyes on the leader, and that the leader gives direction that is easy to follow. Tempo alterations can greatly enhance the worship experience if done properly or be an unnecessary distraction if done poorly.

List some songs, both new and old, that feature tempo alterations. How, if at all, do they improve the songs?_____

_____

_____

List some songs in which are found musical instructions for tempo that are ignored—or, songs that frequently are sung with tempo alterations that are not designated in the music._____

_____

_____

A final admonition

Believing in God's care and provision when it is not really in doubt is no indication of true faith. Learning to trust in God at all times, particularly bad times, is the hallmark of a true believer. Jesus does not ask us to do as the rich young ruler was required to do — "go and sell your possessions and give to the poor" (Matthew 19:21). But what if He did? Can we really believe we would do as Jesus asked in that situation when we cling as tightly as possible to whatever possessions we have?

Psalm 37:25-26 reads, "I have been young and now I am old, yet I have not seen the righteous forsaken or his descendants begging bread. All day long he is gracious and lends, and his descendants are a blessing." The one who trusts in God knows his noble and giving attitude may require him to lean on the Lord a bit more, but he knows the Lord is worthy of his confidence.

Lesson 4

Teach Us How to
ENDURE

Who do you think of when you think of endurance?

Whose face do you see?

Knowing that the testing of your faith produces endurance.
James 1:3

Life comes with hardships. Whether ours are greater or less than those of our neighbors or brethren is not the point; the only issue is whether we have the courage and strength to endure. And far too often, we fail the test. In such times we like to blame the test—it was too much for us, it was unreasonable, it came at just the wrong time, etc. But if we believe Paul's words in 1 Corinthians 10:13, that we will be provided with "the way of escape also, so that you will be able to endure it," blaming the test is tantamount to blaming the God who claims to be sovereign over the test.

The person of faith realizes the key to endurance is not changing the circumstances of life or making excuses for our failures, but rather finding the inner strength to persevere. The "break" we pray for or think we deserve may never arrive; in fact, our circumstances, like many suffering saints who have gone before, may indeed get worse.

The writer of Hebrews encourages his readers to "remember the former days, when, after being enlightened, you endured a great conflict of sufferings, partly by being made a public spectacle through reproaches and tribulations, and partly by becoming sharers with those who were so treated," and tells them, "do not throw away your confidence, which has a great reward. For you have need of endurance, so that when you have done the will of God, you may receive what was promised" (Hebrews 10:32-33, 35-36). It would be tragic to abandon our life of faith just when we are on the brink of receiving everything we have hoped for.

Who is your person of endurance? Describe the impact his or her attitude has on you and others. _____

_____

_____

What is the greatest strain on your faith? What do you do to endure when the strain seems almost unbearable? _____

_____

_____

About the hymn

John Keble was a prolific writer of spiritual verse, although relatively few of his works were put to music in his lifetime and even fewer remain in common usage. "Sun of My Soul" was originally part of a collection of poems entitled *The Christian Year*, published in 1827. The first poem in the collection is entitled "Morning," and the second, "Evening." Our hymn as it is currently known comprises four verses from "Evening." Considerable debate arose as to which verses to include when efforts were made to put the poem to music. Keble himself suggested the song begin a verse later, omitting the verse that now gives the song its name.

JOHN KEBLE

Keble, a modest and unassuming man, published *The Christian Year* anonymously, but its popularity did not allow it to remain anonymous for long. *The Christian Year* went through 109 editions before Keble's death in 1866. Keble was appointed to the Chair of Poetry at Oxford University in 1841 in large measure because of *The Christian Year*. Keble's sermon at Oxford on "National Apostasy" is credited with beginning a movement throughout England to increase spiritual awakening. Keble College at Oxford, established in 1869, is named for him. "Hursley," the name of the tune we know that accompanies Keble's words, is the name of Keble's final parish, where he is buried.

"Hursley" is attributed to Peter Ritter and was arranged for "Son of My Soul" by William Henry Monk in 1861. Monk was the musical editor of *Hymns Ancient and Modern*, which became one

WILLIAM HENRY MONK

of the best-selling hymnals of all time. He composed the music for numerous hymns, the most familiar of which is probably "Abide with Me."

What do you like or not like about this hymn? _____

_____

_____

Share with the class another older hymn that has a similar theme. Do you think this hymn does a better or worse job of teaching us about endurance than "Sun of My Soul"? Explain your answer. _____

_____

_____

_____

Sun of My Soul

1. Sun of my soul, Thou Sav - ior dear, It is not night if Thou be near;
2. When the soft dews of kind - ly sleep My wea - ried eye - lids gen - tly steep,
3. A - bide with me from morn till eve, For with - out Thee I can - not live;
4. Come near and bless us when we wake, Ere thro' the world our way we take,

O may no earth - born cloud a - rise To hide Thee from Thy ser - vant's eyes.
Be my last tho't, how sweet to rest For - ev - er on my Sav - ior's breast.
A - bide with me when night is nigh, For with - out Thee I dare not die.
Till in the o - cean of Thy love We lose our - selves in heav'n a - bove.

Words: John Keble
Music: "Hursley," *Katholisches Gesangbuch*, arr. William H. Monk

F - 3 - DO

About the lyrics

Sun of my soul, Thou Savior dear,
It is not night if Thou be near;
O may no earthborn cloud arise
To hide Thee from Thy servant's eyes.

A common image in hymns is to depict either life in its entirety or life on earth in Christ in terms of a single day. Progressing through life's morning and midday, we consistently and joyfully draw toward day's end, when we will be united with the Lord. Jesus Himself used such imagery in John 9:4—"We must work the works of Him who sent Me as long as it is day; night I coming when no one can work."

Jesus is the sun in the life of a Christian. He gives light, warmth and direction to all who walk in His light. We pray for Him to abide with us "from morn till eve." And when "kindly sleep" (death) finally overtakes us, we close our eyes in anticipation of an even greater fellowship that will be ours when "we lose ourselves in heav'n above."

What are some other songs that use day/night imagery to depict our relationship with Jesus in this life? State which of these songs are most effective in conveying that image, and why._____

_____

_____

_____

What other songs describe death as sleep? Is this a scriptural image? Does the image imply that the soul is temporarily or permanently inactive after death?

_____

_____

_____

About the music: 3/4 time

1. Sun   of   my s
2. When the soft d

In 3/4 time, a quarter note gets one beat. Three beats compose a measure. Because there are only three beats, the first beat is the only one that is emphasized. This lends a smooth, stately rhythm to the song. This is why "waltz time" is so frequently used in music intended for dancing.

The tendency with 3/4 time often is to sing slowly. And it is true that more lively tunes are more likely to be written in 6/8 or 9/8 time. But the actual timing for music in 3/4 time is generally the same as with 4/4 time; it's just that a measure only gets three beats instead of four. Most songs with "waltz" in the title are not slow songs. Listening to recordings of songs such as "The Blue Danube Waltz" by Richard Strauss and "Minuet in G" by Johann Sebastian Bach will give a general idea of the tempo the writer has in mind when he wrote a song in 3/4 time.

List some songs that are written in 3/4 time. Are some typically sung more quickly or slowly than others, and why? _____

_____

_____

"Amazing Grace" is written in 3/4 time, but it is almost always sung much slower than typical waltz tempo. Discuss the problems that may arise when a very familiar song is sung more quickly than customary. _____

_____

_____

_____

Lesson 4A

Teach Us How to
ENDURE EVEN MORE

Be faithful until death, and I will give you the crown of life.
Revelation 2:10

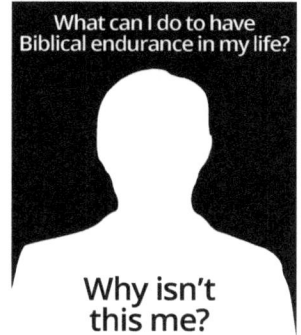

What can I do to have
Biblical endurance in my life?

**Why isn't
this me?**

We are pushed to our limit. We stare despair and doubt in the face. And we choose to drive it back. We emerge with our faith and morality intact. Our faith has been tested (2 Corinthians 13:5), and we have passed.

So it's over, right? Back to business as usual now?

No, unfortunately we find that one trial typically leads to another trial, and then another one after that. These are not irregularities in an otherwise harmonic existence under God's sun. These are the regularities. Our situations are not the trials; *life itself is the trial.* And the secret to survival is not to just hold our breath, grit our teeth, and ride the storm out until it passes. The secret is to realize the storm will never pass. It may increase or lessen in severity from day to day, but it will always blow, beating against our ship of faith, trying to capsize it and drown us in the same ocean that has overwhelmed the vast majority of our neighbors.

We are not entitled to a peaceable existence in this life. We should pray for circumstances that will lead to "a tranquil and quiet life" (1 Timothy 2:2), but tranquil is relative. If the government chooses not to imprison us for our faith or disrupt our worship, we are blessed. But hardships are certain to come from other directions. "Indeed, all who desire to live godly in Christ Jesus will be persecuted" (2 Timothy 3:12). And that is not even considering the regular rigors of life that increasingly take their toll throughout life.

People of faith do not derive confidence from signs of improvement in this life. They derive confidence from God's promise of another, better life to come.

What is the worst thing you have seen happen to a Christian? How did it impact his or her faith? _____

_____

Is your life easier or harder in the Lord than it was five years ago? Ten years? Twenty? Has your attitude toward hardship changed over time?

_____

_____

_____

About the hymn

Craig Roberts is a professor at the University of Missouri and serves as an elder with the Eastside church of Christ in Columbia, Missouri. He serves on the Sumphonia board of directors. Sumphonia produces the hymnal *Psalms, Hymns and Spiritual Songs* as well as a supplemental hymnal. Sumphonia also produces hymn recordings. Roberts has written many hymns in common usage, including "The Greater Light," "Loved Ones," "God of Prayer," and "High above the Seraphim." Roberts is the author of *A Good Hymn*, a resource for hymn writers, and conducts the annual Hymninar in Columbia for hymn writers and aspiring hymn writers.

Roberts wrote the three stanzas with three friends in mind, each of whom were going through particular trials in life. The threefold nature of God's superiority—all-powerful, all-present, all-knowing—seemed to demonstrate His ability to provide comfort in any and every situation of need for His people.

Richard Morrison is an elder with the Spring Valley church of Christ in Plano, Texas. He was an editor of *Sing to the Lord!*, a hymnal composed almost entirely of songs written by students and teachers at the R.J. Stevens Singing School. He also heads up the Gospel Music School of Texas and the website www.songsofthechurch.org, which facilitates the circulation and use of new and unpublished hymns.

Morrison and Roberts met at the R.J. Stevens Singing School; Morrison was a composition teacher and Roberts a student. Both now teach frequent classes in hymn writing.

What do you like or not like about this hymn? _____
_____
_____

Share with the class another newer hymn that has a similar theme. Do you think this hymn does a better or worse job of teaching us about endurance than "Are You Weighed Down?" Explain your answer. _____
_____
_____
_____

About the lyrics

> *For in the midst are gathered two:*
> *All-present God is there with you.*

Matthew 18:20 has often been used as an assurance to believers that their assemblies, even if they comprise only two or three, are still recognized by God. Certainly this is a

Are You Weighed Down?

1. Are you weighed down with cares of life? Weak in temp-ta-tion, faint in strife?
2. Are you a - lone and far a - way? Find a calm place to sing and pray,
3. Are you a - fraid of com-ing years? Filled with un-cer-tain joys and tears?

Lean on the Lord to help you through; Al-might-y God will strength-en you.
For in the midst are gath-ered two: All - pre - sent God is there with you.
Bless-ings or bur-dens, great or few— All-know-ing God knows best for you.

Words: C. A. Roberts
Music: Richard L. Morrison
© 1993 Kelly and Jo Hersey

Ab - 3 - DO

true sentiment, as God is always with His people, whether they are in large crowds, small groups or even alone; the same stanza in "Are You Weighed Down?" implies the presence of God in the life of the believer who is "alone and far away." Small groups should not be discouraged by their smallness; Christ knew the faith of the Smyrna church was not indicated by their tribulation and poverty, nor was the faith of the saints in Philadelphia defined by the "little power" (which would seem to indicate small numbers) they had and would soon exercise (Revelation 2:9, 3:8).

That being said, the efficacy of "small worship" is not in the context of Matthew 18:15-20. Jesus is emphasizing the authority to be exercised in local churches. Those who intervene on behalf of an erring brother in a group of two or three are acting on behalf of the Lord. The fact that two or three witnesses, all of whom love and serve the Lord, can prayerfully agree in a common witness to sin is testimony that they are acting, as Jesus says, "in My name." The judgment they reach will be a reflection of the Lord's will for the lives of the individual and the church; thus He says, "Truly I say to you, whatever you bind on earth shall have been bound in heaven; and whatever you loose on earth shall have been loosed in heaven."

What comfort can be gained from the company of faithful brethren upon whom we can lean in times of trial? _____

_____

_____

_____

Describe the blessings of serving an "almighty," "all-present," and "all-knowing" God. _____

_____

_____

About the music: prayer songs

Song worship leaders should try to construct a worship service in such a way as to tie the various elements together as much as possible. That often involves choosing a song to put the congregation in a proper place for what will follow. Since singing is the part of our worship that requires the most activity from us, singing is uniquely suited to assist in this process.

It is a relatively common practice to include a prayer in the middle of the song service. Worship leaders often choose to lead into the prayer with a prayer-themed song. Songs that speak of prayer, or even that have "pray" or "prayer" in the title, are obvious choices. "Sweet Hour of Prayer," I Will Pray," and "Did You Think to Pray?" are good examples.

However, congregations in the habit of selecting a "prayer song" can fall into the habit of leading the same ones repeatedly, perhaps causing them to lose their impact. The song need not mention the word "pray" prominently, or at all, to accomplish the purpose, which is to put the members in a contemplative mood as they collectively consider God's active role in our lives as Christians. All sorts of songs fit this general category, including "Are You Weighed Down?"

List some songs that could easily be read as prayers. ("Nearer, Still Nearer" is an example.)_____

_____

_____

Many prayer-themed songs include an "Amen" at the end which is often omitted. Do you have feelings one way or the other as to whether it should be sung along with the rest of the hymn? _____

_____

_____

A final admonition

It is easy to get so caught up in our own difficulties that we forget about the difficulties of others. Often the hardships of our neighbors are even worse than our own, but whether they are greater or lesser than our own is not the point. We are commanded to think of others as being more important than ourselves, and of others' interests before our own (Philippians 2:3-4). And those admonitions are not conditional or situational. That means we should be mindful of others regardless of our own personal state.

Seeking opportunities to serve others in their difficult circumstances is a good way of getting our mind off our own problems, and perhaps putting them in proper perspective. By helping others endure hardship, we may accidentally find a way to work through our own.

Lesson 5

Teach Us How to
PRAISE

Enter His gates with thanksgiving and His courts with praise.
Psalms 100:4

Who do you think of when you think of praise?

Whose face do you see?

> *Praise God, from whom all blessings flow!*
> *Praise Him, all creatures here below!*

Two more perfect lines of poetry have never been written. More to the point, those two lines beautifully encapsulate the obligation and privilege we have as His special creation to approach Him in prayer and acknowledge Him as the Giver of "every good thing given and every perfect gift" (James 1:17).

Praise is generally associated with joy. The psalmist writes, "Shout joyfully to the Lord, all the earth; break forth and sing for joy and sing praises" (Psalm 98:4). James 5:13 teaches that the singing of praises should be the natural instinct of the joyful heart— no doubt because our great and praiseworthy God is the One who has brought the joy to us. Ideally, joy should lead to praise, which should remind us further of the Source of our joy, which should prompt even more praise.

For whatever reason, praise does not come easily to many of us—praise either of our fellow humans or our Creator. Perhaps we do not want to elevate someone else above ourselves. Perhaps we feel inadequate or jealous. In any case, particularly with regard to praise of God, it is difficult to see such reluctance as anything other than a display of egotism and pride. Surely none of us truly believes we deserve all, or even most, of the credit for the blessings that have come to us. If that is so, we should be grateful—and we should express that gratitude in such a way as to give honor to the ones, or One, responsible.

In short, if you do not feel "in the mood" to praise God, praise Him anyway. Hopefully the "mood" will follow your actions.

Who is your person of praise? Describe the impact his or her attitude has on you and others. _____

_____

_____

Does the singing of songs of praise put you in a better mood? Why or why not?

_____

_____

About the hymn

RICHARD STORRS WILLIS

The origin of "Fairest Lord Jesus" is confused. Some say it or a near version of it was sung as the "Crusader's Hymn" by knights marching toward Jerusalem in the 12th Century. Another popular story features the followers of John Hus, a Protestant reformer; while being chased out of Bohemia toward Silesia in modern-day Poland, the refugees are said to have buoyed their spirits by dwelling on the glory of God's nature through which they were traveling instead of the circumstances that had forced their migration.

German Jesuits came upon the song and published it in their *Munster Gesangbuch* in 1677, although the words were said to be 15 years older. The story of the Silesian migration fits with the first modern appearance of the hymn. Hoffman Fallersleben heard a group of Silesians singing the hymn and included it in his *Schlesische Volkslieder* in 1842.

The first appearance of the English translation likely was in Richard Storrs Willis' *Church Chorales and Choir Studies* in 1850. Willis is perhaps best known for writing the music for "It Came upon a Midnight Clear." A notation in Willis' book stated the hymn was sung by German Crusaders, perhaps giving rise to the tradition regarding the hymn's earliest roots.

Two stanzas are generally omitted in modern hymnals. They are included here:

All fairest beauty, heavenly and earthly,
Wondrously, Jesus, is found in Thee;
None can be nearer, fairer or dearer,
Than Thou, my Savior, art to me.

Beautiful Savior! Lord of all the nations!
Son of God and Son of Man!
Glory and honor, praise, adoration,
Now and forever more be Thine.

The hymn also appears in some places as "Beautiful Savior" and includes the traditional three verses, with some alterations, as well as this first verse:

Beautiful Savior, King of creation,
Son of God and Son of Man!
Truly I'd love Thee, truly I'd serve thee,
Light of my soul, my Joy, my Crown.

What do you like or not like about this hymn? _____

_____

_____

Fairest Lord Jesus

1. Fair - est Lord Je - sus, rul - er of all na - ture,
2. Fair are the mead - ows, fair - er still the wood - lands,
3. Fair is the sun - shine, fair - er still the moon - light,
4. All fair - est beau - ty, heav - en - ly and earth - ly,
5. Beau - ti - ful Sav - ior! Lord of all the na - tions!

O Thou of God and man the Son,
Robed in the bloom - ing garb of spring;
And all the twin - kling star - ry host;
Won - drous - ly, Je - sus, is found in Thee;
Son of God and Son of Man!

Thee will I cher - ish, Thee will I hon - or,
Je - sus is fair - er, Je - sus is pur - er,
Je - sus shines bright - er, Je - sus shines pur - er
None can be near - er, fair - er or dear - er,
Glo - ry and hon - or, praise, ad - o - ra - tion,

Thou my soul's glo - ry, joy and crown.
Who makes the woe - ful heart to sing.
Than all the an - gels heav'n can boast.
Than Thou, my Sav - ior, art to me.
Now and for - ev - er more be Thine.

Words: German Folk Hymn
Music: Traditional, arr. Richard S. Willis

E - 4 - DO

Share with the class another older hymn that has a similar theme. Do you think this hymn does a better or worse job of teaching us about praise than "Fairest Lord Jesus"? Explain your answer. _____

_____

_____

_____

About the lyrics

> *Fair is the sunshine, fairer still the moonlight,*
> *And all the twinkling starry host:*
> *Jesus shines brighter, Jesus shines purer,*
> *Than all the angels heav'n can boast.*

One of the most frequent metaphors in the Bible is that of darkness and light—darkness symbolizing ignorance and sin, light symbolizing Divine guidance and righteousness. Two songs already discussed, "Joyful, Joyful, We Adore Thee" and "Sun of My Soul," utilize this figure.

It is not difficult to imagine why the pagans often worshiped celestial bodies. The sun provides illumination by day, and the moon and stars provide light, direction and wonder by night. Jesus' superiority to the glories of heaven and earth, to say nothing of pagan deities, becomes more manifest the closer we draw to Him. No matter how attractive the "wisdom" from another source may be, nothing can compare to what we receive from the Lord, and nothing that contradicts what we receive from the Lord is truly "light" at all.

The song also makes use of the dual use of the phrase "heavenly host." The stars are the "host of heaven" (Deuteronomy 17:3) created to glorify God, but that also were worshiped as gods themselves (2 Kings 17:16). But God's army of spiritual warriors is also called His "host" (Joshua 5:14); this is undoubtedly what is meant when God is repeatedly called "Lord of Hosts" (1 Samuel 1:3, Psalm 46:7, etc.).

Worship of angels is strictly forbidden (Colossians 3:18). There is a reason John is rebuked for falling at the feet of an angel (Revelation 22:8-9) and not when he falls at the feet of Christ (Revelation 1:17). Only God is worthy of worship.

Name another song that describes God or Jesus in terms of sunlight. Describe in your own words why sunlight evokes images of God. _____

_____

_____

_____

Do the "extra" verses of "Fairest Lord Jesus" add to or detract from the song as a whole? Explain your answer. _____

_____

_____

_____

About the music: staggered rhythms

Typically all four parts (or however many there may be) of a song sing the same rhythm at the same time. Thus, following along with the leader's rhythm (who is typically singing the soprano part) is generally correct regardless of which part one is singing.

Occasionally, though, the rhythms vary slightly from part to part. The most frequent example of this is the use of a series of quarter notes in the support parts, particularly the bass, with the melody employing dotted quarter notes paired with eighth notes. An example of this is in the third measure of "Fairest Lord Jesus." The sopranos have the melody, as usual; the first syllable of the word "ruler" has a dotted quarter note, requiring it to be held for a beat and a half. All the other parts have a normal quarter note, meaning they will sing the second syllable of "ruler" a half-beat before the melody.

Notice also the soprano and alto tones, which are normally on the same note stem, separate here. When the parts break, the stem facing upward is always the note for the sopranos (or the tenors) and the stem facing downward is always the note for the altos (or the basses)—even on the rare occasion that the upward-facing note is lower on the staff than the downward-facing one.

Also you may notice that the tenors begin the song in the first measure with a half note and the basses have two quarter notes. In these cases also, the notes will occupy separate stems—the one pointing upward for the higher part (the tenor here) and the one pointing downward for the lower (bass).

Find another song that features staggered rhythms. Do you find singing these songs particularly difficult? Do you think the irregularity adds anything to the musical quality of the song? _____

_____

_____

Lesson 5A

Teach Us How to
PRAISE EVEN MORE

*Praise the Lord! Sing to the Lord a new song, and His praise
in the congregation of the godly ones."*
Psalm 149:1

What can I do to have
Biblical praise in my life?

Why isn't
this me?

Does praise lose its sincerity with time and repetition?
Is it possible to "grow weary in well-doing" (to borrow a
phrase from Galatians 6:9)? Some might argue from the other direction — that the
question should be whether praise might possibly not lose its sincerity. Surely we
have all experienced how the same compliment paid dozens or even hundreds of
times —a husband for his wife's cooking, an employer for an employee's work product,
etc. — can become tired and rote.

We may subscribe to the "less is more" philosophy, feeling a small amount of praise in
select settings has more impact than a steady stream of compliments and accolades
that may grow shallow or lose their effectiveness. That may have an element of truth.
However, one would likely be hard-pressed to find a wife or employee (or anyone else,
for that matter) who would not, all things being equal, prefer more praise to less.

Perhaps the easiest way to keep our praise of God from becoming stagnant, as with
praise in other contexts, is to vary the way it is expressed. This is relatively easy in
prayer, when we are choosing our own words. It is more difficult with songs of praise,
as the words are chosen for us by the hymn writer and the worship leader. Even so,
we can exercise some initiative. We can examine the content of the words ahead
of time. We can exhort leaders to avoid wearing certain songs out with over-usage.
Most of all, we can dwell heavily on the words as we sing them to make sure we "sing
with the mind" (1 Corinthians 14:15).

Surely, though, praising God less often is the least acceptable option of all.

**What is keeping you from praising God more effectively? Share with the class
if you are comfortable doing so.**_____

_____

**What other tactics can we use as individual singers to make sure our praise is
effective and heartfelt?**_____

_____

_____

About the hymn

O.E. "Sam" Landrum wrote about 250 songs in collaboration with R.J. Stevens. "O Magnify My Master" was one of their first. Other favorites include "Visions of Calvary," "Broken for Many," and his wife Bernice's favorite, "Gleams the Harvest." A collection of 169 of their hymns, *Songs to Edify*, is in print.

SONGS TO EDIFY

Landrum thinks of his hymns as poetry first. He wrote the lyrics and conceived the melody, then Stevens did the arrangement and harmonies. They met when Stevens was preaching at the Stonegate church of Christ in the Port Arthur, Texas, area, not far from the Landrums' home in Silsbee, Texas. Soon afterward the Landrums began attending the annual R.J. Stevens Singing School in Wilburton, Oklahoma. They quickly became fast friends, habitually calling each other "brother" instead of by name.

Bernice gives Michael Stringer the credit for popularizing "O Magnify My Master" and bringing her husband to broader attention as a hymn writer. Stringer, an accomplished musician and song director as well as a close friend of Stevens, took to bringing paper copies of Landrum's hymns with him when he would visit various congregations to conduct song services. Quickly Christians all over the country and the world were growing to love Landrum's work as much as Stringer.

Stevens and Landrum spoke on the telephone almost every morning after Stevens' final heart attack that wound up leading to his death in 2012. Landrum's own health began to deteriorate almost immediately after Stevens' passing; Bernice thinks his decline may have been connected to the loss of his dear friend. At the time of this writing Landrum still lives in Silsbee with Bernice.

What do you like or not like about this hymn? _____
_____
_____

Share with the class another newer hymn that has a similar theme. Do you think this hymn does a better or worse job of teaching us about praise than "O Magnify My Master"? Explain your answer._____
_____
_____
_____

O Magnify My Master

1. O mag - ni - fy my Mas - ter; Ex - alt His ho - ly name.
2. With words of ad - o - ra - tion, With songs of end - less praise,
3. As well as I may praise Thee In my own frag - ile way,

His name I praise for - ev - er, For - ev - er and a - gain.
From hearts that know but glad - ness, For love of heav - en's ways;
Nor with my soul, O Je - sus, Could I Thy love re - pay.

To heights of all Thy glo - ry, To heights be - yond the sky,
And from yon realms, ma - jes - tic, Where saints of ag - es gone,
I sing of all Thy grac - es; I bow and laud Thy care,

To far be - yond cre - a - tion, to Him let prais - es fly.
With joy my soul would cher - ish, Praise Je - sus all day long.
And take of all Thy bless - ings. I see them ev - ery - where.

Words: Onice Landrum
Music: Onice Landrum, arr. R. J. Stevens
© 1998 Onice Landrum and R. J. Stevens

F - 4 - MI

About the lyrics

As well as I may praise Thee in my own fragile way.
Nor with my soul, O Jesus, could I Thy love repay.

Reading poetry is not like reading prose. Sentence structure is likely to be twisted, words omitted or slightly misused, and definitions stretched. Sometimes this makes the song more thought-provoking; sometimes it just makes it more confusing. But if "He who searches the heart knows what the mind of the Spirit is" (Romans 8:27), surely improper grammar will not separate a worshiper from his or her God.

The first two lines of the third verse of "O Magnify My Master" do not, technically and grammatically, form sentences. But the thoughts behind the words are clear. In singing them we say we are offering Jesus whatever feeble words (including ungrammatical ones!) we may manage, but that no offering of worship up to and including the offering of our very soul could balance the scales after what He has done for us.

Although we can and should be willing to mull over lyrics for a time to discern the thoughts behind them, a thought in a song can become so convoluted as to make it unreasonably difficult to sing with a worshipful attitude. Leaders should exercise judgment in this regard while choosing songs for the congregation. A word or two of instruction before singing may be helpful; feeling the need to do much more than that is likely an indication that the song is a poor choice.

List some other songs with awkward phraseology. How much does it disturb you to sing these songs? How much of the blame for confusion should rest on, respectively, the hymn writer, the leader, and yourself?_____

_____

_____

_____

Are there any songs in the hymnal you currently use that you feel are doctrinally objectionable? If so, explain your opposition._____

_____

_____

_____

About the music: opening songs

The first song of a song worship service accomplishes many purposes beyond the obvious ones of "teaching and admonishing." As the song is frequently near the beginning if not at the very begging of the worship, a song's tone and tempo can set the mood for the entire service. Therefore it is advisable to choose a song that is well known to the group, that moves quickly, and that tends to inspire positive emotions in the participants.

Many Bible prayers, including the "Lord's Prayer" itself, begin with praise. Often in our enthusiasm for songs that motivate and inspire Christians to proper, godly behavior, we almost forget the most important half of our audience; we are making melody "to the Lord" while we are "speaking to one another" (Ephesians 5:19). This motivates many song worship directors to lead at least one song of praise at the top of the program. And since songs of praise tend strongly to be quickly paced and encouraging in their tone, choosing a song of praise accomplishes both purposes equally well.

What does it mean to praise God? Why do we do it in song? _____
_____
_____

What happens to the group, and to you as an individual worshiper, when an inappropriate song begins the song worship? How much is the worship leader to blame for this? _____
_____
_____

A final admonition

A significant part of our worship, both public and private, should be devoted to praise. Jesus was in the habit of praising His Father (Matthew 11:25, John 17:1-5). Paul praised God in his written prayers (Romans 11:33-36, Ephesians 3:20-21). Surely this constitutes a pattern for us to follow.

One way to develop a habit of praise is to insert the word "praise" in our prayers where we might ordinarily use the word "thank." Hebrews 13:15 reads, "Through Him then, let us continually offer up a sacrifice of praise to God, that is, the fruit of lips that gives thanks to His name." This is in keeping with the prayers we see frequently in the Psalms. Psalm 92:1-2 is an example: "It is good to give thanks to the Lord and to sing praises to Your name, O Most High; to declare your lovingkindness in the morning and Your faithfulness by night." It may seem artificial at first, or even pointless. But the habit needs to start somehow, some way. If we begin with praising Him in our prayers, we soon may find ourselves praising Him in all facets of our lives as is indicated in Psalm 89:1—"I will sing of the lovingkindness of the Lord forever."

Lesson 6

Teach Us How to

LOVE

Who do you think of when you think of love?

Whose face do you see?

We know that we have passed out of death into life, because we love the brethren.
1 John 3:14

Preachers like to show off their Greek knowledge when the subject of love arises. *Agapeo* love looks like this, *phileo* love looks like that, and such like. But the bottom line is, love is not a complicated concept. As 1 John 4:7-8 states, "Brethren let us love one another, for love is from God, and everyone who loves is born of God and knows God. The one who does not love does not know God, for God is love." God loves perfectly; if you want to learn love, learn to think and act like God.

The classic verse with regard to God's love, of course, is John 3:16—"For God so loved the world, that He gave His only begotten Son, that whoever believes in Him shall not perish, but have eternal life." Obviously we will not have opportunity to give a child for the world. But it is easy, and humbling, to understand how important a relationship with us was to Him. In loving Him, and in loving our brethren, we must desire that relationship just as much.

The most important part of expressing love, and probably the most difficult, is selflessness. To "love your neighbor as yourself" (Matthew 22:39) is to value and pursue his interests as enthusiastically and consistently as you do your own. That's a tall order. But if we can learn to do this, including for people who do not show any real interest in loving us, then "you are to be perfect [in love], just as your Heavenly Father is perfect" (Matthew 5:48).

Who is your person of love? Describe the impact his or her attitude has on you and others. _____

_____

_____

How does God's love for us impact our dealings with others?_____

_____

_____

_____

About the hymn

CHARLES WESLEY

Charles Wesley and his brother, John, are credited for founding Methodism. He and John were partners in preaching for almost all their adult lives, with John being more known for the oratorical word and Charles for the lyrical.

Charles Wesley, by any standard, must be considered one of the greatest hymn writers, if not the greatest, of all time. He wrote a full 623 of the 770 hymns in the Wesleyan Hymn Book. It is thought that he wrote more than 6,500 hymns in all. Dozens of them remain in great usage today among people of widely varying doctrinal stripes. Examples include "A Charge to Keep I Have," "Love Divine," "Hark, the Herald Angels Sing," "Jesus, Lover of My Soul," and "Soldiers of Christ, Arise."

"And Can It Be?" was written shortly after Charles Wesley's own public commitment to Christ on May 21, 1738. The newness of his faith is demonstrated in the wonder he expresses in his lyrics, particularly the first verse. It is thought that "And Can It Be?" was sung three days later, perhaps as a chant, at his brother John's conversion ceremony.

The tune traditionally associated with "And Can It Be," called "Sagina," was written by Scottish poet and composer Thomas Campbell in 1835. Campbell, who has no connection to the Campbells of the "Restoration Movement" in America, died in France in 1844 and is buried in Westminster Abbey in London.

A different tune, credited in some places to Bob Kauflin, has also been paired with Wesley's lyrics over the years. It is Darrell Bledsoe's arrangement of the newer tune that appears in this book.

What do you like or not like about this hymn? _____
_____
_____
_____

Share with the class another older hymn that has a similar theme. Do you think this hymn does a better or worse job of teaching us about love than "And Can It Be?" Explain your answer. _____
_____
_____
_____

And Can it Be?

1. And can it be that I should gain An in - t'rest in my Sa - vior's blood?
2. You left Your fa - ther's throne a - bove— So free and in - fi - nite Your Grace—
3. Bold - ly I come be - fore Your throne, To claim Your mer - cy im - mense and free.

Died He for me who caused His pain, For me who scorned His per - fect love?
Emp - tied Your - self of all but love, And bled for A - dam's help - less race.
No great - er love will e'er be known, For, O my God, it found out me.

CHORUS

A - maz - ing love! How can it be That You, my God, would die for me?

A - maz - ing love! How can it be That You, my God, would die for me?

Words: Charles Wesley, arr. Bob Kauflin and Darrell Bledsoe
Music: Bob Kauflin, arr. Darrell Bledsoe

F - 4 - DO

About the lyrics

You left Your Father's throne above, so free and infinite Your grace;
Emptied Yourself of all but love, and bled for Adam's helpless race.

The obvious problem with using hymns written by people from a denominational background (or, for that matter, hymns written by any human beings at all) is that they may reflect teaching not grounded in Scripture. Regardless of the hymnist's background, lyrics should be examined for their truthfulness beyond all. It is quite likely, especially with a denominational hymn, that it may give the impression of false doctrine to some singers without stating anything that is actually unscriptural. Singers should not feel that the attitude of the hymnist is being accepted and promoted when we sing his lyrics.

The idea of Jesus dying for "Adam's helpless race" is an example. Wesley no doubt believed in the inherited depravity of man. But there is nothing incorrect about the helplessness of mankind in the absence of a Savior: "For while we were still helpless, at the right time Christ died for the ungodly" (Romans 5:6). One need not believe in "original sin" or any related theory to sing this line in faith.

A great deal of debate has raged over the idea of how Jesus "emptied Himself" (Philippians 2:7). Emptied Himself of what? And for what purpose? The Scriptures clearly teach Jesus did not "empty Himself" of His Divine nature, as Paul describes Him as "the fullness of Deity . . . in bodily form" (Colossians 2:9). He Himself claimed to be Deity multiple times and in multiple ways while in the flesh—"He who has seen Me has seen the Father" (John 14:9), for instance. If a singer can sing this line thinking of Jesus divesting Himself of His heavenly home and the trappings of Deity but not His actual Divine nature, he or she should not be concerned if others may be reading more than that into the song.

In what sense did we cause Jesus' pain on the cross? _____

_____

_____

_____

How and when do we come before Jesus' throne to claim "mercy immense and free"? Is any action other than prayer necessary from us? _____

_____

_____

_____

About the music: Lord's Supper songs

One of the most common tactics song worship leaders use is to use a song to set the mood for the partaking of the Lord's Supper. The usual approach to take is to select a song that describes either the Supper itself or Jesus' suffering on the cross.

Some songs, though, deal with the motivations behind the cross—love and grace prominent among them. Likewise, songs that emphasize our attitude toward Christ (love, appreciation, thankfulness) can be effective in turning our hearts and minds toward the Supper.

"And Can It Be?" addresses the cross briefly, but most of the attention is paid to the general topic of God's grace and love, and our own worthlessness. Most hymnal editors provide a topical index; several headings in the index may direct a song worship leader to songs that would be appropriate to use in this way.

Find other hymns that might not deal directly with the cross or the Supper, but that might be effective as Lord's Supper preparation songs. Discuss their appropriateness._____

_____

_____

Find a song, either new or old, unknown to you that would be effective as a Lord's Supper song. Discuss the song's meaning._____

_____

_____

Lesson 6A

Teach Us How to
LOVE EVEN MORE

May the Lord cause you to increase and abound in love for one another.
1 Thessalonians 3:12

What can I do to have Biblical love in my life?

Why isn't this me?

Most of the accomplishments for which we strive are not of the "check the box" variety. Generally they are qualities that make us more Christlike in our thoughts and behaviors, and they are expected to grow throughout our walk with Jesus throughout life.

Love is certainly an example of this. Paul writes in 1 Thessalonians 4:9-10, "Now as to the love of the brethren, you have no need for anyone to write to you, for you yourselves are taught by God to love one another; for indeed you do practice it toward all the brethren who are in all Macedonia. But we urge you, brethren, to excel still more." Brotherly love is a natural, even inevitable, result of the Spirit working in the child of God. But we can adopt an attitude that fosters, retards, or even reverses this love. As we will never in this life fully achieve the sort of love God has for us, we always have room for improvement. Therefore, if we are God's children, we must always be improving.

The "holy kiss" of Romans 16:16 has been likened to a handshake in the modern day. That may not convey the idea effectively; often we shake hands with people in our culture specifically because we do not know them. Our greeting, whatever cultural form it may take, needs to carry with it the connotation of brotherly love—pure in its nature, genuine in its expression, constant in its demonstration. Merely making sure to speak to, or even wave at, every church member may or may not demonstrate love. It's not about the action itself; it's about the look on our face and the tone in our voice when we perform the action.

For whom do you have trouble expressing love? Why is that? _____

_____

_____

What can we do on a weekly basis to demonstrate love for the brethren?

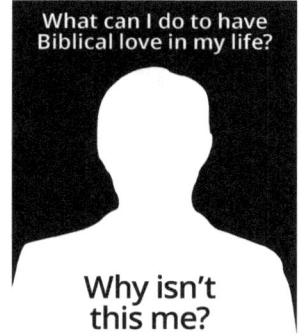

_____

_____

_____

What is Love?

1. O, what is love? A soft frag-ile thing;
2. A moun-tain high with clouds in the haze,
3. The love of God is good and so kind;

It's hard to say words that make your heart sing;
Per-haps sun-light beams a-cross gold-en blades;
It pa-tient-ly waits, no e-vil in mind;

A gen-tle breeze, a soft sum-mer rain,
A way to live, a way to sur-vive,
Love bears all things; re-joic-es in truth;

A rose with dew, a walk in the lane.
Be-cause our God is so much a-live.
Its faith and hope will make the heart sing.

God is love! God is light! God is pow-er! Yes, God is might!

Words: Jean L. McBride, st. 3, R. J. Stevens
Music: Gerald L. McBride, arr. R. J. Stevens
© 1996 Gerald & Jean L. McBride

D - 3 - MI

About the hymn

Gerald McBride is a retired construction worker in Summerville, Tennessee. His fondness for guitar playing fit well with his wife Jean's affinity for poetry. Jean, who passed away in October 2013, took up verse late in life, putting secular and spiritual thoughts alike in poem form. "What Is Love?" particularly got Gerald's attention, and, thinking it might make a good song, composed a melody for it on the guitar.

The McBrides met R.J. Stevens in a gospel meeting in Lawrenceburg, Tennessee. Jean, without telling Gerald about it, handed the song to Stevens, who liked it immediately, added the third verse to re-emphasize the spiritual nature of love, and arranged it for four-part harmony. The song became circulated very quickly among churches, singing meetings and camps. It was first published in *Sing to the Lord!* in 2002, and then in *Hymns For Worship (Supplement)*. It remains the only song by the McBrides in print.

What do you like or not like about this hymn? _____
_____
_____

Share with the class another newer hymn that has a similar theme. Do you think this hymn does a better or worse job of teaching us about love than "What Is Love?" Explain your answer. _____
_____
_____
_____

About the lyrics

> Oh, what is love? A soft fragile thing;
> It's hard to say words that make your heart sing;
> A gentle breeze, a soft summer rain,
> A rose with dew, a walk in the lane.

Much of "What Is Love?" does not read as prose; rather, it often simply piles images upon one another for the purpose of creating a mood. The rather confused structure of the song is very effective in expressing the author's difficulty in putting the concept of love into words. Then, as the song reaches the chorus, it is as if the author has found the proper words—"God is love!"

The love of God is best manifested in the words of the Bible, and particularly in the gift of His Son for our sins (John 3:16). But the observer of nature and of life can see signs of God's care and devotion to mankind in the smallest of details. As with an earthly father who brings joy to his children with the smallest acts of attention and kindness, so also God shows His love for us in the little things of life that are no less beautiful for their smallness—"a rose with dew, a walk in the lane."

These things, it should be noted, do not cease when we falter in our faith. Indeed, "He causes His sun to rise on the evil and the good, and sends rain on the righteous and the unrighteous" (Matthew 5:45). The faithless can appreciate a rainbow, for instance, without glorifying God and seeing His mercy represented in it. The faithful, however, have no excuse for such ignorance and ingratitude (Genesis 9:16). We should find God's love demonstrated in hundreds of ways every day, both small and large.

What are some everyday things that bring the love of God to our minds?

_____

_____

_____

Is it possible to appreciate a song for its musicality so much that we ignore the lyrics or rationalize indifferent or even unscriptural lyrics? If so, give examples of songs that strike you this way. _____

_____

_____

_____

About the music: dynamics

Composers often enhance the mood of the song by employing dynamics—that is, variations in volume. Two general instructions are given—*forte* and *piano*, Italian for loud and soft. They are signified in music with the letters *f* and *p*. Sometimes, for extra emphasis, the composer designates *fortissimo* or *pianissimo* (*ff* or *pp*) for extra volume or extra softness, respectively. Sometimes *mezzo forte* (*mf*, a bit softer than *forte*) or *mezzo piano* (*mp*, a bit louder than *piano*) are used to indicate volume closer to the middle of the range.

make your heart sing;
cross gold - en blades;
e - vil   in   mind;

Crescendo (cresc.) and *decrescendo (decresc.)* indicate a gradual increase or decrease in volume. Frequently they appear as two sides of a narrow triangle, with the open end indicating the louder portion and the point indicating the softer portion. Sometimes only the words or abbreviations are used.

"What Is Love?" employs dynamics heavily, making it more interesting and more exciting to sing. Although these are hardly the biggest considerations when choosing a song, they are not irrelevant either. Properly done, making a song softer or louder can draw special attention to the words and enhance their effectiveness. The questions raised in "What Is Love?" about the nature of love and the shallow demonstrations of it in the physical world are answered with emphasis in the chorus—"God is love!" The word "might" at the end of the chorus, sung *fortissimo*, sounds mighty indeed.

Soft singing has a strong tendency to influence the group to slow down and the leader to gradually lower the pitch; the first is seldom advisable, and the second is never advisable. Firm hand direction and eye contact from the leader can help with the first; only practice can help with the second.

List some other songs that make use of dynamics. What impact do dynamics have on the mood of a song?_____

_____

_____

Some song worship leaders may introduce dynamics changes not written in the music. What tactics do some song worship leaders use to do so, and how effective and helpful are they? _____

_____

_____

A final admonition

Love begins with God. We can get so caught up in our expressions of love to our brethren that we forget our "first love" (Revelation 2:4). We should never allow ourselves to think that our attitude toward our brethren defines us completely. Yes, brotherly love is a proof of our discipleship to the world (John 13:35). But we became brethren because we became children of God, not the other way around. Brotherly love is an extension of our love for God.

Personal demonstrations of love for God often are private affairs—prayer, confession, thanksgiving. But they are every bit as real and important as the most public of praises. Our physical parents delight in our presence and want more than anything for us to do the same. Likewise, we must find ways to take pleasure in the presence of God. Allow David to be your example: "When I remember You on my bed, I meditate on You in the night watches, for You have been my help, and in the shadow of Your wings I sing for joy" (Psalm 63:6-7).

Lesson 7

Teach Us How to
STUDY

Your word is a lamp to my feet and a light to my path.
Psalm 119:105

Who do you think of when you think of study?

**Whose face
do you see?**

Singing is not Bible study. But both singing and prayer are, or should be, closely connected to Bible study. The closeness we feel to God upon reading His word finds its expression in our songs. As James 5:13 reminds us, "Is anyone among you suffering? Then he must pray. Is anyone cheerful? He is to sing praises." Just as an acknowledgement of sin in our lives brought on by Bible study should move us to prayer, so also a knowledge of our "participation in the gospel" (Philippians 1:5) should move us to glorify the One who makes all things possible for us.

"Faith comes from hearing and hearing by the word of Christ" (Romans 10:17). And the voices of the faithful naturally rise up before the Lord in worship. But they also retreat back into the word which prompted the faith in the first place. By reciting in music the particulars of our walk with Christ, as found in the Scriptures, we encourage review and further study of such matters in our own study life and in the lives of our brethren.

This is what "teaching and admonishing one another with psalms and hymns and spiritual songs" (Colossians 3:16) is all about. We use the words of others, accompanied by music, to remind ourselves and our brethren of the way in which the Lord says we should go. By no means should we assume the words of a "spiritual song" will bring us closer to Christ; but they certainly should do so if they are rooted in the text and sung with reverence and understanding.

Who is your person of study? Describe the impact his or her attitude has on you and others. _____
_____
_____

What Bible topics tend to be emphasized the most in our songs? Why do you think that is the case?_____
_____
_____
_____

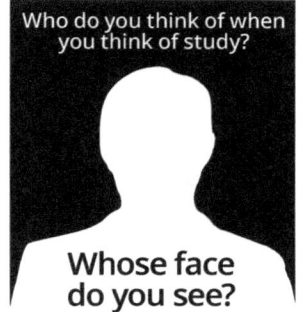

About the hymn

MARY ARTEMISIA LATHBURY

Mary Artemisia Lathbury was the daughter of a Methodist minister, and sister to two others. She herself founded the Look-Up Legion, a Methodist Sunday School organization. She visited Chautauqua, New York, frequently during the summer and soon became affiliated with the Chautauqua Movement, which aimed first to train Bible class teachers but soon spread to incorporate instruction in secular subjects, including entertainment. Theodore Roosevelt called it "the most American thing in America;" Woodrow Wilson deemed it "an integral part of our national defense."

Lathbury was a natural fit for the Chautauqua Movement and joined it quickly after its inception. Soon she became known as the "Poet Laureate of Chautauqua." John Vincent, the founder of the movement, asked her to write a hymn to be sung at Chautauqua Bible studies. While sitting by the bank of Lake Chautauqua in 1877, she was caused to remember the Lord's miracle by the sea and there wrote "Break Thou the Bread of Life." The first two verses of the hymn, as typically sung, are Lathbury's; two extra verses were added in 1913 by Alexander Groves, the first and most popular of which is included here.

WILLIAM F. SHERWIN

More than 60 of Lathbury's hymns were in circulation among churches in the 20th Century; however, "Break Thou the Bread of Life" and "Day Is Dying in the West" are easily the most familiar to most audiences.

The tune was composed the same year by William F. Sherwin. Sherwin was the organizer and director of choirs at Chautauqua from 1874 to his death in 1888. Sherwin, in addition to composing music, also wrote music and lyrics to hymns of his own, the most familiar of which is likely "Sound the Battle Cry."

What do you like or not like about this hymn? _____
_____
_____

Share with the class another older hymn that has a similar theme. Do you think this hymn does a better or worse job of teaching us about study than "Break Thou the Bread of Life" Explain your answer. _____
_____
_____
_____

Break Thou the Bread of Life

1. Break Thou the bread of life, Dear Lord, to me,
2. Bless Thou the truth, dear Lord, To me, to me,
3. Thou art the bread of life, O Lord to me,

As Thou didst break the loaves Be - side the sea;
As Thou didst bless the bread By Gal - i - lee;
Thy ho - ly word the truth That sav - eth me;

Be - yond the sa - cred page I seek Thee, Lord;
Then shall all bond - age cease, All fet - ters fall,
Give me to eat and live With Thee a - bove;

My spir - it pants for Thee, O liv - ing Word!
And I shall find my peace, My all in all.
Teach me to love Thy truth, For Thou art love.

Words: Mary A. Lathbury, st. 3 Alexander Groves
Music: William F. Sherwin

E♭ - 2 - MI

About the lyrics

Beyond the sacred page I seek Thee, Lord;
My spirit pants for Thee, O living Word.

Jesus as the "Word" is a familiar figure in the New Testament, particularly in John's writings (John 1:1, 1 John 1:1, etc.). As God has always communicated His will through incomplete agencies in the past, Jesus is the complete revelation of His will for mankind "in these last days" (Hebrews 1:1-2). A relationship with God necessarily involves a relationship with "the way, and the truth, and the life" (John 14:6)—i.e., the *only* way, truth and life. And a relationship with Jesus is indistinguishable from a relationship with the words of instruction He sent through the Holy Spirit (John 16:13).

But simply knowing information about Jesus, or even accepting that information as fact, should not be enough for the Christian. We seek Him "beyond the sacred page"— through prayer, through introspection, through application of His word in our daily lives. Certainly we cannot come to know anything about Him or the Gospel outside of the Bible; however, a deeper understanding than merely an intellectual one can be had by those whose spirit truly pants for a close and meaningful relationship with their Savior.

The above line has been altered in some places to read, "Within the sacred page I seek Thee, Lord." Do you think this alteration is necessary or advisable?

_____

_____

_____

Is this a "Lord's Supper" song? Why or why not?_____

_____

_____

_____

About the music: sermon songs

Relatively few songs in common usage extol the value of the written word. "Break Thou the Bread of Life" is written in such a way as to emphasize that it is God ultimately, not the preacher, who delivers the word of salvation. The word carried by God's servant 2,000 years after it was delivered has as much apostolic and Divine authority as it ever did, since the word itself remains unchanged.

Some song worship leaders like to use songs of this sort to put the minds of the audience in the right frame for Bible study, much as Lord's Supper songs prepare us for communion with the Lord in His death. Unfortunately, since there are relatively few hymns in this area, the risk is increased of overusing what hymns we have.

List some older hymns that describe the blessing of the written word. _____

_____

_____

What are some other approaches worship leaders can employ to use songs to prepare the audience to receive God's word? Give examples. _____

_____

_____

_____

Lesson 7A

Teach Us How to
STUDY EVEN MORE

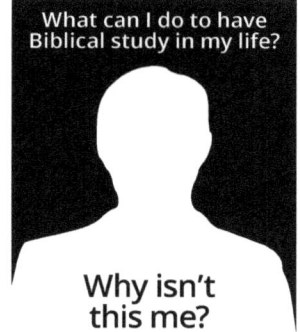

For whatever was written in earlier times was written for our instruction.
Romans 15:4

There are dozens of ways to study the Bible, and all of them are good. Perhaps the least effective, though, is the simple "a chapter a day" or "five minutes a day" approach. Many people employ such techniques to read their way through the Bible, sometimes in a single year. Such is a noble goal in and of itself, and certainly any method of reading the Bible regularly is better than not reading it at all. But simply passing one's eyes over the text is no assurance of internalizing the text's message. We are looking to be aware, informed and motivated through our study. Reading the Bible for form's sake runs the risk of promoting a "check these boxes" approach to study with no assurance of real spiritual growth—which, after all is the whole point (2 Peter 3:18).

Vary your techniques to enliven your study. Read entire books at a sitting—many of them will take no more than ten or fifteen minutes for most readers. Isolate small passages and read them intently; run cross-references to add to your understanding. Use concordances and other tools to study particular words or concepts. Force yourself to read books or texts with which you may be less familiar; vary your approaches to studying them, perhaps including the use of commentaries or study partners, until it becomes more clear.

Most importantly, always be reading, regardless of approach, with the question in mind—*What does this mean for me in my walk with Christ?* Being "an effectual doer" (James 1:25) will help us make the conversion from being a mere student of Jesus Christ to being a true disciple (John 8:31).

Should unforeseen and unfortunate circumstances produce a lack of confidence in God? Why or why not? _____

_____

_____

What is the impact, for good or bad, of trusting in God in our everyday lives?

_____

_____

About the hymn

Charlotte Couchman is a prolific hymn writer who has penned music and lyrics for multiple hymns that have been well received around the country.

Couchman is an editor for the Sumphonia hymnal, *Psalms, Hymns, and Spiritual Songs*. Sumphonia has featured several of her hymns in its recordings, including "How Long Till the Morning?", "The Lord Is My Light," "Sing and Rejoice in the Savior's Birth," and "Triumphal Entrance."

Couchman took inspiration for this hymn from Psalm 119, the classic text regarding the value and glory of God's word. Each verse highlights a different facet of its magnificence, each one supplying joy to the reader; "I have inherited Your testimonies forever, for they are the joy of my heart" (v.111).

The "treasure" aspect of the word is emphasized in verse 11—"Your word I have treasured in my heart, that I may not sin against You." Psalm 19:10 also comes to mind: "[God's words] are more desirable than gold, yes than much fine gold; sweeter also than honey and the drippings of the honeycomb." The "hope" aspect featured in the second verse comes through in verse 49—"Remember the word to Your servant, in which You have made me hope." The emphasis of the third verse on wisdom and guidance appears throughout the psalm, notably in verse 105—"Your word is a lamp to my feet and a light to my path." Comfort and consolation are featured in verse 4, and in verse 156 of the psalm—"Great are Your mercies, O Lord; revive me according to Your ordinances." Finally, the permanence and finality of God's word are seen in verse 89—"Forever, O Lord, Your word is settled in heaven."

"The truth is everlasting," says Couchman, commenting on Psalm 119 and her treatment of it. "No matter what changes come, no matter what is destroyed around us. God's word will prevail."

What do you like or not like about this hymn? _____

_____

_____

Share with the class another newer hymn that has a similar theme. Do you think this hymn does a better or worse job of teaching us about study than "Thy Word Is a Treasure"? Explain your answer. _____

_____

_____

_____

Thy Word Is a Treasure

1. Thy word is a treas-ure, More pre-cious than earth's fine gold.
2. Each page holds a prom-ise: Peace, mer-cy, re-deem-ing love.
3. Thy word is all wis-dom; Thy coun-sel I glad-ly seek.
4. Thy word gives me com-fort When sor-row seems hard to bear,
5. Thy word is e-ter-nal, Though heav-en and earth must end.

How my heart grows rich-er Each time the sto-ry is told!
Each prom-ise ex-alts my Hope to sing prais-es a-bove.
Guide my un-der-stand-ing; O-pen my eyes, LORD, to see.
A song for my jour-ney, Strength when my soul would de-spair.
Thy truth shall en-dure For-ev-er and ev-er. A-men.

Words: C. E. Couchman
Music: C. E. Couchman
© 1986 C. E. Couchman

Db - 2 - MI

About the lyrics

Each page holds a promise: peace, mercy, redeeming love.
Each promise exalts my hope to sing praises above.

Every aspect of God's word has value. Books of history tell of God's treatment of His enemies and His patience with His people. Books of poetry tell us how to sing His praises and seek His counsel. Books of prophecy emphasize His long-term management of the commitment He has made to the faithful, and how He governs in the affairs of men and nations to bring His will to pass. Most importantly, all of them direct us toward the gift of His Son on the cross—either looking forward in the case of Old Testament books, or looking backward in the case of New Testament books. All roads lead to Jesus.

The Bible itself is an implicit promise from God that He will love us and provide for us when we come to Him in faith. He would not have given us a message from His throne if it were not possible for us to hear, believe and apply it. The promises of "peace, mercy, redeeming love" and countless other blessings are as secure as His word. Believing that, because we believe in Him, we become more and more motivated to praise Him for His goodness shown to us here in this life—and more than that, to praise Him for the opportunity that will be ours to glorify Him eternally before His throne in heaven.

Single out two or three verses from Psalm 119 for the joy they bring you as a person of faith. Be prepared to share them with the class. _____

_____

_____

_____

Randomly open your Bible. Find something at that opening that brings praise to God and/or brings you joy as His child. Be prepared to share your discovery with the class. _____

_____

_____

_____

About the music: double flats

We have discussed earlier the concept of accidentals—flats, sharps and naturals. A note receiving a flat is lowered in pitch by a half-step; with a sharp, the pitch goes up a half-step.

Two halves make a whole, obviously. But sometimes the composer thinks adding, for instance, an extra flat to a B note that is already flatted is easier on singers than asking them to just sing an A—especially in a key in which the A is also flatted.

Exactly such a scenario occurs in "Thy Word Is a Treasure." The tenors are asked to sing a "B♭♭" two measures from the end. As is usually the case with double-flatted notes, it provides a downward transition between two notes that are already flatted—in this case, a B♭ and an A♭. Going upward from an A♭ to a B♭ by half-steps, likely the composer would use an A♮ instead.

More rarely, composers will utilize a double-sharp, which looks much like an X. It augments a sharped note upward just as a double-flat augments a flatted note downward. In "Ivory Palaces," the alto part includes double-sharped notes in the chorus. At one place an F♯ is augmented upward with an extra sharp, then downward again with a natural combined with a sharp. The natural alone would erase both sharps, leaving an F♮. The double-sharp, combined with the "natural-sharp," provides the half-step transition the composer intended.

Find other examples of songs with double-sharps or double-flats. _____

_____

_____

A final admonition

James 3:1 reads, "Let not many of you become teachers, my brethren knowing that as such we will incur a stricter judgment." His point is not to discourage teaching but to motivate teachers to take their responsibility seriously. Whether it is an individual speaking to his neighbor, an elder speaking to an erring brother, or a preacher speaking to 10,000 viewers on YouTube, the responsibility is a heavy one and should be borne with caution and prayer.

Choosing to bring the words of a hymnist to the attention of the congregation carries with it the same responsibility as that of a preacher choosing his own words to explain a Bible passage or context. Careful and prayerful study is important. A preacher who would take up a half-hour of the church's attention on a certain line of thought simply because he was in the mood to do so, or because it meant something special to him, without regard to the needs of the group, would be thought shallow and inconsiderate; if his attitude did not change, his status with the church likely would. How is it different for a song worship leader who occupies a half-hour of the church's time simply singing songs he likes to sing, without regard to their effectiveness or even accuracy in presenting the gospel?

The church's worship is in the hands of the song leader for the duration of the song service; if he cannot be trusted to put the needs of the church first, he should not be trusted to do so.

Lesson 8

Teach Us How to

SERVE

The Son of Man did not come to be served, but to serve.
Matthew 20:28

Who do you think of when you think of service?

Whose face do you see?

The most fundamental lesson in practical Christianity is learning to subordinate your own wishes and needs in preference to those of another, and particularly those of Jesus. It is also one of the most difficult to learn and to master. Fortunately, it could not be easier to examine. If the typical decisions being made in your day-to-day life (from how you spend your money and time to how willing you are to pause for pedestrians at a crosswalk) are made primarily on the basis of your own interests, that should be a big red flag.

We have the blessing of four biographies of the greatest Servant of all; Matthew, Mark, Luke and John show us in gripping detail what a true servant looks like. It is perhaps best encapsulated in John 15:13—"Greater love has no one than this, that one lay down his life for his friends." Although Jesus would, just a few hours later, fulfill this statement in the most literal of fashions, that is not the primary point He is making. Jesus laid down His life for His friends not when He went to the cross, but when He came to earth. His entire existence was a blessing to others, from the newlyweds and their family for whom He made wine from water (John 2:1-11) to the grieving Mary and Martha to whom He restored their dead brother, Lazarus (John 11:38-44).

Virtually every impulse we receive in this physical world is to take care of ourselves, first and foremost. It takes faith in the spiritual world, and in a spiritual Lord and Judge, to develop a habit of consistently looking to others before ourselves. But we are assured, "your Father who sees what I done in secret will reward you" (Matthew 6:4) for your selflessness and generosity.

Who is your person of service? Describe the impact his or her attitude has on you and others. _____

_____

_____

Is it appropriate to publicly praise someone for his or her deeds of service? Does that defeat the purpose? _____

_____

_____

About the hymn

ROBERT LOWRY

Robert Lowry was one of the most prolific and popular composers of the 19th century. Yet for all his success as a hymn writer in his lifetime, Lowry preferred to be known as a preacher. He graduated from the University of Lewisburg (now Bucknell University) and was ordained a Baptist minister in 1854. He continued in the ministry until his death in 1899. He also served at a professor and chancellor at Lewisburg and edited 23 volumes of hymns.

Lowry wrote an estimated 500 hymn compositions, including "We're Marching to Zion" and "All the Way My Savior Leads Me"—the latter a collaboration with his frequent writing partner, Fanny J. Crosby. He was also adept at writing lyrics to fit his music, including "Nothing but the Blood," "Watch and Pray," "Shall We Gather at the River?" and "Christ Arose."

SYLVANUS DRYDEN PHELPS

Sylvanus Dryden Phelps was a graduate of Yale Divinity School and spent most of the rest of his life as the pastor of the First Baptist Church of New Haven, Connecticut. He wrote, among other things, a volume of poetry, much of which was in hymn form, entitled *Songs for All Seasons: A Scriptural and Poetical Calendar for Holidays, Birthdays, and All Days*. "Something for Jesus" was, even in Phelps' day, the most familiar and popular work in that collection.

None of Phelps' other works are widely used today; however, Lowry wrote on the occasion of Phelps' 70th birthday,

"It is worth living 70 years even if nothing comes of it but one such hymn as,

'Savior! Thy dying love
Thou gavest me;
Nor should I aught withhold,
Dear Lord, from Thee.'

"Happy is the man who can produce one song which the world will keep on singing after the author shall have passed away. May the tuneful harp preserve its strings for many a long year yet, and the last note reach us only when it is time for the singer to take his place in the heavenly choir."

The lyrics for "Something for Jesus" first appeared in *Watchman and Reflector* in 1864. They were reworked and paired with Lowry's tune in 1871.

Something for Jesus

1. Sav - ior, Thy dy - ing love Thou gav - est Me.
2. Give me a faith - ful heart, Like - ness to Thee,
3. All that I am and have, Thy gifts so free,

Nor should I aught with - hold, Dear Lord, from Thee.
That each de - part - ing day Hence - forth may see
In joy, in grief, through life, Dear Lord, for Thee!

In love my soul would bow, My heart ful - fill its vow,
Some work of love be - gun, Some deed of kind - ness done,
And when Thy face I see, My ran - somed soul shall be

Some of - f'ring bring Thee now, Some - thing for Thee.
Some wan - d'rer sought and won, Some - thing for Thee.
Through all e - ter - ni - ty Some - thing for Thee.

Words: Sylvanus D. Phelps
Music: Robert Lowry

G - 4 - MI

What do you like or not like about this hymn? _____

_____

_____

Share with the class another older hymn that has a similar theme. Do you think this hymn does a better or worse job of teaching us about service than "Something for Jesus"? Explain your answer. _____

_____

_____

_____

About the lyrics

> *Give me a faithful heart—likeness to Thee—*
> *That each departing day henceforth may see*
> *Some work of love begun,*
> *Some deed of kindness done,*
> *Some wand'rer sought and won,*
> *Something for Thee.*

Our service to Jesus shows itself in our service to others. Jesus Himself said as much (Matthew 25:41-46). As 1 John 3:17 reminds us, "But whoever has the world's goods, and sees his brother in need and closes his heart against him, how does the love of God abide in him?" When we reach out in kindness toward our neighbor, we are not just showing our compassion for him; we are showing our devotion to Christ and our desire to have the heart and mind He had (Philippians 2:5).

Jesus assures us as a gesture as simple as "a cup of cold water" will show us to be His people and assure us of His reward (Matthew 10:42). Anyone who has seen a marathon knows that those engaged in a race that will press them to their limits, who cannot even take a moment to rest, are immensely grateful to see a friend, or even a total stranger, extending them a cup of water to help sustain them for the miles that lie ahead.

How does Jesus "give" us a faithful heart? Is there anything we can or must do to receive such a heart? _____

_____

_____

_____

Share if you can an example where a seemingly small thing done by someone else made a real difference for good in your life. _____

_____

_____

_____

About the music: offering songs

We have discussed the custom of singing a particular song in preparation for the partaking of the Lord's Supper. The collection for the work of the church is not a part of the Supper; yet for convenience's sake it is frequently done at the same time as the Supper, either just before or just after.

Some churches sing a song as a preparation for the collection as well—partially to help separate it from the Supper, partially to "prepare our minds" for this part of our gathering that, as is the case with the Supper, should be done with purpose and premeditation of thought. "Each one must do just as he has purposed in his heart, not grudgingly or under compulsion for God loves a cheerful giver" (2 Corinthians 9:7).

Few if any of our hymns address the collection directly. But several deal with subjects that are directly connected to it. If the song worship leader is asked to choose a song to go with the collection, he should choose an appropriate one.

What topics addressed in spiritual songs are particularly suitable for the collection? _____

_____

_____

List some suitable "collection songs" and explain their suitability. _____

_____

_____

_____

Lesson 8A

Teach Us How to
SERVE EVEN MORE

And be subject to one another in the fear of Christ.
Ephesians 5:21

What can I do to have
Biblical service in my life?

**Why isn't
this me?**

The first trick in adopting the life of a servant is to resign yourself to the fact that you will not get your way as often as you would like, or even as often as your fellow Christian. The second trick, and one even more difficult, is *not minding that you are doing so.*

Among Peter's admonitions designed to help brethren in times of trial bond together instead of tearing the fellowship apart, he writes, "Be hospitable to one another without complaint. As each one has received a special gift, employ it in serving one another as good stewards of the manifold grace of God" (1 Peter 4:9-10). "All that I am and have, Thy gifts so free," Sylvanus Dryden Phelps phrased the blessings of God in the hymn we discussed earlier. Those gifts should not just be used for the benefit of our brethren; they should be used cheerfully and joyfully, knowing we are privileged to do so and that we follow the example of our Master in doing so. Surely there is nothing for a faithful Christian to complain about as he pursues the will of Christ in his own life and lifts up his brethren in the process.

"All things" that are to be done without grumbling or disputing (Philippians 2:14) includes acts of service. After all, what good is it if we act selflessly and then complain about not getting the proper credit for doing so? Such behavior is only self-centeredness "once removed"—little or no better than undisguised, unrepentant egotism. No, we do as Christ commands—as Christ Himself did; then we accept with humility whatever praise that comes, and we refuse to be discouraged by whatever praise does not come.

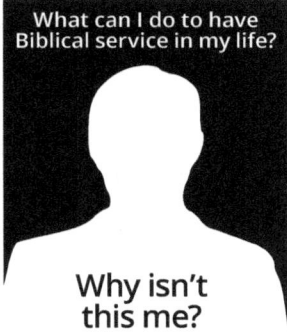

Should we try to avoid being seen by third parties as we serve? _____
_____
_____

What should we do if we see the pattern of service we are trying to set ignored by our brethren? _____
_____
_____

About the hymn

Tim Jennings is the preacher for the Spring Creek church of Christ in Plano, Texas, where Richard Morrison serves as an elder. During a series of lessons on servanthood, an older member of the congregation remembered singing a song called "Make Me a Servant" that his mother had sung to him in his youth but that had not ever seen it in a hymnal or supplement. Jennings reworked the lyrics and Morrison the music, and then Morrison arranged the song, which then consisted of the first verse only.

Feeling the theme deserved fuller treatment, Morrison enlisted the aid of Matthew Bassford. Bassford, who was a member at Spring Creek during his high school years, quickly wrote two more verses to form the hymn as it exists now.

Bassford now is a preacher for the Joliet church of Christ in Joliet, Illinois. He has written dozens of songs in common usage, including "Rejoice and Sing That God Is Great!", "Savior and Friend," and "Exalted." He is a technical editor for the *Psalms, Hymns and Spiritual Songs* hymnal, and he blogs on spiritual music and other related themes at www.hisexcellentword.blogspot.com.

What do you like or not like about this hymn? _____
_____
_____

Share with the class another newer hymn that has a similar theme. Do you think this hymn does a better or worse job of teaching us about service than "Servant Song"? Explain your answer. _____
_____
_____
_____

About the lyrics

Make me a servant, just like Your Son,
For He was a servant; please make me one.

The first line of the old song was, "Make me a servant, Lord, make me like You, for You are a servant; make me one, too." Tim Jennings changed the object of the request from Jesus to the Father because of some debate in the congregation over whether it is appropriate to address Jesus directly in song. (The question is similar to the issue of directing prayer toward Jesus, as discussed elsewhere in this book.)

Of course, God does not "make" anyone anything. We allow Him to transform us when we allow His word to renew our minds (Romans 12:2). When the gospel splits us open

Servant Song

1. Make me a ser - vant, Just like Your Son.
2. Make me a ser - vant; Take all my pride,
3. Make me a ser - vant, Filled by Your might,

For He was a ser - vant, Please make me one.
For I would be low - ly, Hum - ble in - side.
And may all my la - bors Shine with Your light.

Make me a ser - vant, Do what You must do
Giv - ing to oth - ers With all that I do;
Show me Your foot - steps And what I should do;

To make me a ser - vant, Make me like You.
In love for my broth - er, Make me like You.
For now and for - ev - er, Make me like You.

Words: Jimmy and Carol Owens, arr. Tim Jennings and Matthew W. Bassford F - 3 - MI
Music: Jimmy and Carol Owens, arr. Richard L. Morrison
© 1978 Communiqué Music, In.; st. 2-3 © 2000 Tim Jennings

before God (Hebrews 4:12-13), we have an opportunity to look inside ourselves as well. And if we see our service lagging behind, a godly attitude will compel us toward improvement—"for it is God who is at work in you, both to will and to work for His good pleasure" (Philippians 2:13).

Certainly Jesus should be our example in everything (1 Peter 2:21); in no area is He a better example, or a more needful one, than in the area of servitude.

The last line of Jennings' version of the song seems to have God the Father portrayed as a servant—a role typically given to Jesus. Is it proper to think of our Father as our servant? Explain why or why not. _____

_____

_____

_____

List some passages that demonstrate the servant attitude of Christ. Describe how we can use these passages to stimulate servitude in ourselves and others.

_____

_____

_____

About the music: invitation songs

The choosing of an invitation song can become almost mindless; the most obvious signs are when songs such as "Oh Why Not Tonight?" and "Are You Coming to Jesus Tonight?" are sung during daytime services. (Most of us have witnessed such occurrences more than once.)

Familiarity is the best and the worst trait of an invitation song. Arguably, the meaning of an invitation song is more important than that of any other song, since it is particularly aimed at bringing a lost soul to Jesus. Therefore it is even more important than usual that the song be familiar to the vast majority of the group and to the sinner himself. However, singing the same eight or ten invitation songs constantly can rob them of their meaning; singing a song by rote can be as ineffectual for the lost soul as not singing it at all.

Hymns for Worship (Revised) lists more than 70 songs in its topical index under the heading of "Invitation." Most of them would be considered "standards" by the majority of churches. That means a congregation could sing a different invitation song for months on end with no repeats. Also, many songs not traditionally used in this part of the worship service will suit it very well; using them in a different aspect of worship than usual might lend their meaning extra emphasis. Any song that emphasizes the need for repentance and transformation (like "Servant Song"), or the greatness of our Savior and our salvation, or the need for commitment from us as Christians may be a suitable invitation song, and song worship leaders should be encouraged to examine them for use as such.

What are your favorite "invitation songs?" Why these ones? (Consider factors beyond "I like it" or "We sing this one a lot.") _____

_____

_____

Name some songs not usually used for invitations that would be suitable.

_____

_____

_____

Many "invitation songs" feature questions in the title and throughout the hymn. What sort of questions should we be asking a sinner as a sermon draws to a close? _____

_____

_____

_____

A final admonition

Perhaps the greatest illustration of servitude in the text is in John 13, where Jesus washes the feet of His disciples, and then says in verses 14-15, "If I then, the Lord and the Teacher, washed your feet, you also ought to wash one another's feet. For I gave you an example that you also should do as I did to you." His point was not that the literal washing of feet would be or should be a tradition among Christians, but that His disciples should not ever think so highly of themselves that they hesitate to act in service toward one another, no matter how degrading and undignified we may find that expression of service to be.

He says in the very next verse, "Truly, truly, I say to you, a slave is not greater than his master, nor is one who sent greater than the one who sent him." He says virtually the same thing to His disciples later on that evening (John 15:20) and on at least two different earlier occasions (Matthew 10:24, Luke 6:40). The point is obvious: If it was not beneath the dignity of our Lord and Savior to commit Himself to service while in the flesh, it should not be beneath our dignity either.

Lesson 9

Teach Us How to
HOPE

And now, Lord, for what do I wait? My hope is in You.
Psalm 39:7

Who do you think of when you think of hope?

Whose face do you see?

Countless generations of Christians have buoyed their spirits in difficult times by reminding themselves that better times were coming, and then bolstering that hope by reading the assurances found in God's word. Solomon writes in Proverbs 24:13-14, "My son, eat honey, for it is good, yes, the honey from the comb is sweet to your taste know that wisdom is thus for your soul; if you find it, then there will be a future, and your hope will not be cut off." The more wisdom we take from God, the sweeter our life becomes—even if the actual circumstances of that life do not improve, or even if they worsen.

The people of the world hope in this life alone. That pushes them to put more effort into accomplishment within their lifetime than we as Christians are prepared to exert—especially when those efforts push them in ungodly directions. Their success in this life, which often and predictably exceeds our own, can grate at us. We see ourselves, and rightly so, as more deserving; we may even convince ourselves that a loving, righteous God would not permit such to be so. Before long we are wresting the Scriptures to rationalize a carnal approach to life that diminishes our service. We have lost our hope.

The knowledge and wisdom we are to seek in this life begins with "the fear of the Lord," as we are told countless times in the wisdom literature (Job 28:28, Psalm 111:10, Proverbs 1:7, etc.). Therefore, as Solomon exhorts in Proverbs 23:17-18, "Do not let your heart envy sinners, but live in the fear of the Lord always. Surely there is a future, and your hope will not be cut off."

Who is your person of hope? Describe the impact his or her attitude has on you and others. _____

_____

_____

What can we do to take our minds off the worries and concerns of this life and redirect them toward heavenly things?_____

_____

_____

Blessed Assurance

1. Bless - ed as - sur - ance, Je - sus is mine!
2. Per - fect sub - mis - sion, per - fect de - light,
3. Per - fect sub - mis - sion, all is at rest;

Oh, what a fore - taste of glo - ry di - vine!
Vi - sions of rap - ture now burst on my sight;
I in my Sav - ior am hap - py and blest,

Heir of sal - va - tion, pur - chase of God,
An - gels de - scend - ing bring from a - bove
Watch - ing and wait - ing, look - ing a - bove,

Born of His Spir - it, washed in His blood.
Ech - oes of mer - cy, whis - pers of love.
Filled with his good - ness, lost in His love.

Words: Fanny J. Crosby
Music: Phoebe Palmer Knapp

D - 3 - MI

About the hymn

Frances Jane Crosby—or "Aunt Fannie," as she came to be known to the world—was born on March 24, 1820. When six weeks old when she developed an eye affliction. A traveling doctor prescribed a mustard poultice that cured the infection but created scarring that rendered her permanently sightless. Despite her disability, she quickly developed a knack for poetry; the first lines she wrote were these:

O what a happy soul I am,
Although I cannot see,
I am resolved that in the world
Contented I will be.
How many blessings I enjoy
That other people don't!
To weep and sigh because I'm blind,
I cannot, and I won't.

FRANCES JANE CROSBY

She told her mother she would not accept her sight back even if it were possible—"for when I die, the first face I see will be of my blessed Savior."

She had memorized large sections of the Bible by the age of 10. She also learned the piano, harp and organ. She became a lifelong activist for the blind; while lobbying in Washington she met a young Grover Cleveland, who was working for the Institute for the Blind. She became close friends with the future U.S. president, also meeting several other presidents during her storied life. Hers was the first female voice ever heard on the floor of the Senate in Washington. By the time of her death, she was thought to be the most famous woman in America.

She did not write her first hymn until she was 45. William B. Bradbury, the composer for hymns such as "Jesus Loves Me," "Just As I Am" and "Sweet Hour of Prayer," had become discouraged by the quality of church hymns. He was immediately drawn to Crosby's talents and employed her in the labor of lyric writing. Although Bradbury died in 1868, Crosby's association with his company lasted more than forty years.

By the time of her death in 1915 at the age of 95, she had written 8,000 hymns, making her almost certainly the most prolific hymn writer of all time. Her hymns remain among the most popular in the world a century after her death; favorites include "God Be With You," "He Hideth My Soul," "I Am Thine, O Lord," "Near the Cross," "Praise Him, Praise Him," "Rescue the Perishing," and "Tell Me the Story of Jesus."

She said late in life about her blindness:

It seemed intended by the blessed providence of God that I should be blind all my life, and I thank him for the dispensation. If perfect earthly sight were offered me tomorrow I would not accept it. I might not have sung hymns to the praise of God if I had been distracted by the beautiful and interesting things about me.

When her friend Phoebe Knapp brought one particular tune to her, she listened to it two or three times and said, "It says to me, 'Blessed assurance, Jesus is mine, O what a foretaste of glory divine.'" Those words, immortalized in one of her most beloved hymns of all, were placed on a large marker forty years after her death by "friends to whom her life was an inspiration." Her original, far more modest headstone simply reads, "She hath done what she could."

Ira Sankey, whose revival meetings helped bring Crosby to national and international attention, wrote the following of her impact on the lives of people:

> "During the recent war in the Transvaal," said a gentleman at my meeting in Exeter Hall, London, in 1900, "when the soldiers going to the front were passing another body of soldiers whom they recognized, their greetings used to be, 'Four-nine-four, boys; four-nine-four;' and the salute would invariably be answered with 'Six further on, boys; six further on.' The significance of this was that, in 'Sacred Songs and Solos,' a number of copies of the small edition of which had been sent to the front, number 494 was 'God be with you until we meet again;' and six further on than 494, or number 500, was 'Blessed Assurance, Jesus is mine.'"

What do you like or not like about this hymn? _____
_____
_____

Share with the class another older hymn that has a similar theme. Do you think this hymn does a better or worse job of teaching us about hope than "Blessed Assurance"? Explain your answer. _____
_____
_____
_____

About the lyrics

Blessed assurance, Jesus is mine;
O what a foretaste of glory divine!
Heir of salvation, purchase of God,
Born of His Spirit, washed in His blood.

Being "born again" (John 3:3) provides the Christian the confidence that not only is his life aimed toward God in this life, "glory divine" awaits as well. The blessings we receive as children of God on earth are mere foretastes of what is to come.

Christians are "heirs of salvation" in the sense that we have not yet received the full blessing our Father has to give us; we yet stand to receive the bulk of our inheritance.

Jesus gives us "the Holy Spirit of promise, who is given as a pledge of our inheritance, with a view to the redemption of God's own possession, to the praise of His glory" (Ephesians 1:13-14). Having already purchased us with His blood (Acts 20:28, Revelation 5:9, etc.), Jesus provides the Spirit to lead us (Romans 8:14); seeing His will for us as revealed in the text lived out in our own lives provides testimony to our salvation and inheritance (Romans 8:16-17).

The hope we have in Jesus is not blind hope or false hope; it is hope made sure by the word of God Himself—"blessed assurance" indeed!

Does singing about the "assurance" of our salvation make you more convinced of it? Does it minimize at all the possibility of apostasy?_____

_____

_____

Describe in your own words what you think "glory divine" is._____

_____

_____

_____

About the music: compound rhythms

Typically the "beat" of a song is signified by the beat of the director's hand; that is, in 3/4 time, the director would beat three times per measure. Some music, however, is written in compound time; that means each "beat" represents several notes instead of just one.

"Blessed Assurance" is written in 9/8 time. That means an eighth note gets a beat, nine of them per measure. But following the director for nine beats in every measure would be excessively difficult for the audience (to say nothing of the strain it would put on the director). Thus the song is typically directed with three beats instead of nine, with each beat representing three eighth notes.

Other common examples of compound rhythms include 6/4, 6/8 and 12/8. For 6/4 and 6/8 time the director typically gives only two hand motions per measure—6/4 typically being paced a bit more slowly than 6/8. A 12/8 piece of music receives four hand motions per measure. All of these, you will note, result in a single motion representing three beats. The grouping of notes in threes this way tends to lend a lilting air to the music, much like you would find in music written in 3/4 time.

Find more songs that feature different compound rhythms. Practice beating time to your songs and others' songs using the compound rhythm beat pattern.

_____

_____

Lesson 9A

Teach Us How to
HOPE EVEN MORE

And hope does not disappoint, because the love of God has been poured out within our hearts.
Romans 5:5

What can I do to have Biblical hope in my life?

Why isn't this me?

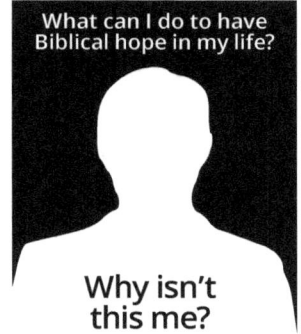

Circumstances of this life are constantly pushing us to reevaluate our priorities as Christians. What we hope for in the next life is not as pressing as what we need, or think we need, in this life; Satan knows that, and he pressures us with all his tactics to, if only temporarily, forget about the life that is waiting for us after this one. But minutes turn to hours, and then to days, and before long we have forgotten our hope entirely.

Worse yet, we can become convinced that the miseries of this life are somehow a reflection on God, a demonstration that He is not mindful of us and our hardships, perhaps even evidence that He does not exist at all.

The very nature of hope demands that we look toward that which we cannot see. We should remember, as hopeful beings, that the state of affairs here has nothing to do with heaven, any more than rain at home means rain on the other side of the world.

When trials come, and they will come, we must lean on our hope instead of abandoning it. Paul writes in Romans 5:3-5, "we rejoice in our tribulations, knowing that tribulation brings about perseverance; and perseverance, proven character; and proven character, hope; and hope does not disappoint, because the love of God has been poured out within our hearts through the Holy Spirit who was given to us."

"The hope of His calling" (Ephesians 1:18, "the hope of the gospel (Colossians 1:23), "the hope of salvation" (1 Thessalonians 5:8) was never intended to be seen in anything resembling its fullness in this life. We should not be discouraged when we have trouble seeing it through the haze of this life; we should be reminded to look even harder for it.

What causes Christians to lose their hope? What can we do to keep from losing our own? _____

_____

What glimpses of heavenly glory can see from here on earth? _____

_____

_____

About the hymn

I go through phases with my musical tastes. One week I found myself listening, almost compulsively, to Celtic Woman. The traditional Irish music, full of images of loss and home and departure struck an emotional chord with me, to the point that I became almost uncontrollably sad for the better part of two office days.

I am a firm believer that the writer should go in the direction that the creative process takes him. That week it was poetry. "My Crossing" was complete within a couple of hours, almost exactly the way it appears here.

MIKE ROGERS

I posted it on a Facebook group page frequented by hymn writers and asked if anyone wanted to try putting music to the words. In that way I became acquainted with Mike Rogers, an adjunct professor of music theory at Dallas Baptist University. Mike is a director involved with the Praise & Harmony hymn recording series, and has written several pieces that appear on their recordings, including a new arrangement of "Rock of Ages." Rogers was a total stranger to me with whom I had never even exchanged Facebook messages before "My Crossing." He volunteered for the project and finished the project in less than a day. The entire creative process was complete in less than 36 hours.

Upon first hearing the music, I immediately thought Mike must have been in my head. The tone of the music was very much like the Irish music that had inspired the hymn in the first place.

What do you like or not like about this hymn? _____

_____

_____

Share with the class another newer hymn that has a similar theme. Do you think this hymn does a better or worse job of teaching us about hope than "My Crossing"? Explain your answer._____

_____

_____

About the lyrics

Come my child, and build with me
Vessel yours to cross the sea.
With you long I may not be,
For I make my crossing.

My Crossing

1. Star - ing out a - cross the sea I hear an - gels call to me,
2. As my boat I rea - dy make, Sor - rows of this land for - sake,
3. Oth - er bur - dens here I find, Weigh - ing down my heart and mind.
4. En - e - mies of flesh and soul, Wear at sail and deck and hull,
5. Come, my child, and build with me Ves - sel yours to cross the sea.

Speak - ing of what soon will be When I make my cross - ing.
Earth - ly ties I yearn to break So to make my cross - ing.
Weep - ing, pray - ing, I, re - signed, Wait to make my cross - ing.
Wres - tling me to gain con - trol For to stop my cross - ing.
With you long I may not be, For I make my cross - ing.

pp rit.

When I make my cross - ing.
So to make my cross - ing.
Wait to make my cross - ing.
For to stop my cross - ing.
For I make my cross - ing.

Words: Hal Hammons
Music: Mike Rogers
© 2014 Hal Hammons and Mike Rogers

D - 3 - DO

I have two daughters. Parents (and other role models) of faith try to instill that faith in the younger generation, but ultimately it is the choice of the individual whether or not to believe. Time is limited, and we must find ways to utilize however much or little of it we may have.

Children of Christians may make the mistake of assuming their own faith is strong because their parents' faith appears to be; their parents may make the same assumption. Perhaps the best way to check is for the parent to help the child pass the test of 1 Peter 3:15—"but sanctify Christ as Lord in your hearts, always being ready to make a defense to everyone who asks you to give an account for the hope that is in you, yet with gentleness and reverence." If a child is able to respond to Bible questions with confidence instead of doubt, with humility instead of braggadocio, that is a good sign.

What are some ways we can share our hope in Christ with others? _____
_____
_____

What are some questions we can ask ourselves and others to confirm that our hope is strong and stable?_____
_____
_____

Do you find songs about death difficult to sing? Which ones particularly, and why? _____
_____
_____

About the music: themes

The notion of a hymn writer using his personal experience and background to forge his lyrics goes back all the way to David gazing at the stars and writing Psalm 8 or sitting in the pasture with his sheep while writing Psalm 23, as I imagine him doing. Of course, David had Holy Spirit guidance to help him shape his words, but every indication throughout Scripture is that the writers' own backgrounds—whether it be Paul's personal associations, John's memories, or the patriarchs' family histories—were used by the Spirit in assembling the text.

Themes are essentially the musical equivalent of parables—an extended series of figurative images designed to help the reader (or in this case, the singer) connect to the thoughts more effectively.

Nautical themes are one of the most common in our hymnody. Sailors far from home and facing death and the unknown every day were naturally caused to look to God for protection and guidance; putting oneself in the position of such a sailor is an easy way to be reminded of our reliance on God. Farming and warfare are other themes that frequently lend themselves to the expression of spiritual thoughts, both in the inspired text and in our hymns.

What is your favorite nautical hymn? Your favorite farming hymn? Your favorite warfare hymn? Why these? _____

_____

_____

_____

It has been suggested by some that hymns written in previous centuries, using images and comparisons that are foreign to most singers today, have outlived their usefulness. Do you agree or disagree? Explain._____

_____

_____

_____

A final admonition

It is easy to become caught up in the day-to-day, year-to-year concerns of our life here on earth. But if in so doing we neglect our hope of heaven, we endanger our eternal future and that of those who look to us for guidance. It is not enough to convince ourselves we have heaven in our hearts; for us to be an influence for others, we must have heaven in our hands and on our lips.

Imagine yourself building a boat named *Hope*. In it you plan to travel to heaven. How much time do you spend working on it? How diligently do you check it for leaks? Can you imagine yourself climbing aboard and actually setting sail in it? Would your neighbor, brother or child know what a boat is supposed to look like, or how to properly build one, by watching you?

Lesson 10

Teach Us How to
FIGHT

Some boast in chariots and some in horses, but we will boast in the name of the LORD, our God.
Psalm 20:7

Who do you think of when you think of the Christian fight?

Whose face do you see?

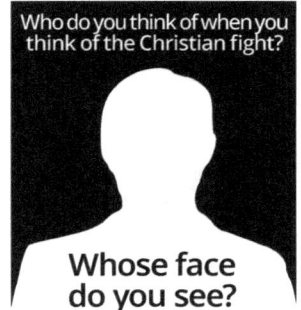

The vast majority of humankind tries to avoid fighting—and desperately hopes the vocal and bellicose minority manage to occupy themselves with each other. But Paul's admonition in Romans 12:18—"If possible, so far as it depends on you, be at peace with all men"—implies that conflict will be unavoidable at times. The question in such times is not whether the fight will occur; it is whether we will engage the fight that is brought to us and, if so, how we will do it.

The devil may declare cease-fires from time to time, but he never observes them. War was declared in the Garden of Eden, and it has waged ever since. His "flaming arrows" (Ephesians 6:16) are always in the air and headed in our direction. And if we are not wearing "the full armor of God" that the same text describes, we are setting ourselves up for failure—perhaps a fatal one. A single "flaming arrow," depending on how, when and where it strikes, may be all it takes to destroy us.

If Satan is always looking for us, "seeking someone to devour" (1 Peter 5:8), we should be always looking for him. He may come "in sheep's clothing" (Matthew 7:15). He may come from our own brethren, even our own leadership (Acts 20:29-30). But we, like Elisha's servant of old, are surrounded by unseen spirit warriors, ready to come to our aid in our conflict with evil (2 Kings 6:15-18). Truly, "those who are with us are more than those who are with them."

The outcome of this war has already been determined. It was known before the foundation of the world. The only remaining bit of drama is what side we will be on in the end.

Who is your person of fighting? Describe the impact his or her attitude has on you and others. _____

_____

_____

How do we "contend without being contentious"?_____

_____

_____

About the hymn

Isaac Watts, born in 1674, was brought up a religious Nonconformist. His refusal to accept traditional religion as practiced by the Church of England showed an attitude of innovation and forward thinking that would forever change the way hymns were sung.

Watts is known as the "Father of English Hymnody." He is credited with 750 hymns, dozens of which remain in usage today. Favorites of his include "When I Survey the Wondrous Cross," "At the Cross," "O God, Our Help in Ages Past" and "We're Marching to Zion."

ISAAC WATTS

Watts, like no other hymn writer in the English language before him, introduced new poetry into the hymnody. He also proposed that the Psalms should be reworked to fit a Christian philosophy rather than that of the Old Testament. "Joy to the World," his adaptation of Psalm 98, is perhaps the best known example of this treatment.

Watts, who served as pastor of the Independent Church in London from 1702 until his death in 1748, is said to have written "Am I a Soldier of the Cross?" in conjunction with a sermon he had prepared on 1 Corinthians 16:13—"Be on the alert, stand firm in the faith, act like men, be strong."

He was also well known in his day for his secular writings. His treatise on logic went through twenty printings; his "Against Idleness and Mischief" is quoted in *David Copperfield* by Charles Dickens, writing a century after Watts' death.

Thomas A. Arne is credited for "Arlington," the music used in "Am I a Soldier of the Cross?" He is best known for composing "Rule, Brittania!" the *de facto* musical theme of the British Empire in the 18th and 19th centuries. He wrote "Arlington" in 1762; the complete hymn first appeared in 1784, in Ralph Harrison's *Sacred Harmony—a Collection of Psalmtunes, Ancient and Modern.*

What do you like or not like about this hymn? _____

_____

_____

Share with the class another older hymn that has a similar theme. Do you think this hymn does a better or worse job of teaching us about love than "Am I a Soldier of the Cross?" Explain your answer. _____

_____

_____

_____

Am I a Soldier of the Cross?

1. Am   I   a   sol - dier   of   the   cross,   A   fol - l'wer   of   the   Lamb,
2. Must   I   be   car - ried   to   the   skies   on   flow - 'ry   beds   of   ease,
3. Are   there   no   foes   for   me   to   face?   Must   I   not   stem   the   flood?
4. Sure   I   must fight   if   I   would reign;   In - crease   my   cour - age, Lord.
5. Thy   saints,   in   all   this   glo - rious   war,   Shall con - quer, though they die;
6. When that   il - lus - trious day shall   rise,   And   all   Thine   ar - mies shine

And   shall   I   fear   to   own   His cause   Or   blush   to   speak His name?
While oth - ers fought to   win   the prize   And   sailed through blood - y   seas?
Is   this   vile world   a   friend   to   grace   To   help   me   on   to God?
I'll   bear   the   toil,   en - dure   the   pain,   Sup - port - ed   by   Thy word.
They   see   the   tri - umph from   a - far,   By faith's   dis - cern - ing   eye.
In   robes of   vic - t'ry through the skies,   The glo - ry   shall   be Thine.

Words: Isaac Watts
Music: "Arlington," Thomas A. Arne, arr. Ralph Harrison

G - 3 - DO

About the lyrics

Must I be carried to the skies
On flow'ry beds of ease,
While others fought to win the prize,
And sailed through bloody seas?

How arrogant is it of us to require of God favorable circumstances and limited hardships as a condition of our discipleship? What soldier is allowed to decide for himself what battles are to be fought, what risks are to be run, what hazards are to be faced?

God does not owe us any consideration. He does not owe us anything; it is we who owe Him. Therefore we are obligated to serve Him in whatever way He deems fit, and to praise Him for the opportunity to do so.

It is particularly inappropriate for us, in comfortable circumstances, to complain about what little amount of adversity we do face. The Bible is replete with examples like "Antipas, My witness, My faithful one who was killed among you, where Satan dwells" (Revelation 2:13). Watts' "bloody seas" may evoke images of the conflict between good and evil in Revelation, including the souls beneath the altar in Revelation 6:9-11 who "deserved better treatment" every bit as much as we do—"men of whom the world was not worthy" (Hebrews 11:38)—and suffered fates far worse than we can imagine.

"Is this dark world a friend to grace, to help me on to God?" Watts asks rhetorically in the third stanza. Why should we expect fair treatment from our worldly neighbors, or complain when we don't get it? The sooner we identify our allies and enemies, the sooner we can start responding to each accordingly.

Under what circumstances might we "fear to own His cause"? _____
_____
_____
_____

Are there ever fights with the world that are not worth fighting? Explain.
_____
_____
_____

About the music: closing songs

We have all exited a gathering of the saints singing or humming a song from that service; many of us do it weekly. It's a demonstration of how music can get into our minds and stay there long after the final note fades. The blessing for us is, the words of the songs may linger with us as long and as deeply as the music.

That is part of the thought process behind "closing songs"—a hymn sung, generally in conjunction with a prayer, to signal the end of worship. Because this song is sung last, it is the one most likely to stick in our minds; song worship leaders have an opportunity, then, to extend the impact of the worship service long after the final "Amen" by choosing an appropriate song. On the other hand, choosing an unfamiliar, difficult or otherwise inappropriate song can leave the worshiper with a bad taste in his mouth, despite the best efforts of the leader, the preacher, and the other congregants.

The most important consideration, as is typically the case, is content. The song should encourage contemplation and application of God's word—particularly the aspect of the word emphasized in the worship service. Leaders may coordinate with the preacher to find an appropriate song to "go out on." Depending on the way a service is structured and announced, it may be appropriate to change the closing song at the last minute to fit the service.

The song need not be "peppy" to inspire and excite the audience, but it should not drag. "Be With Me, Lord," "God Be With You" and similar hymns can be very effective in this role, but not if half the audience is put to sleep.

How appropriate is "Am I a Soldier of the Cross" as a closing song? What could be done to make it more or less appropriate? _____

_____

_____

What are your favorite "closing songs?" Why these ones? (Consider factors beyond "I like it" or "We sing this one a lot.") _____

_____

_____

_____

Discuss the appropriateness of the following songs as closing songs: "Now the Day Is Over," "The Lord Bless You and Keep You," "The New Song," and "An Evening Prayer."_____

_____

_____

_____

Lesson 10A

Teach Us How to
FIGHT EVEN MORE

I have fought the good fight, I have finished the course, I have kept the faith.
2 Timothy 4:7

What can I do to have Biblical warfare in my life?

Why isn't this me?

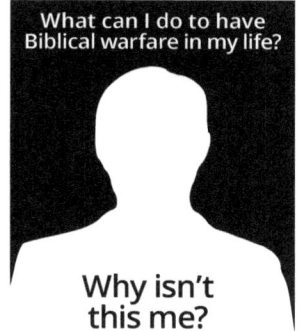

Pogo said decades ago, "We have met the enemy, and he is us." He could just as easily have had reference to the people of God, more's the pity. Despite confessions to the contrary, many Christians have more of the world in them than they have of Jesus Christ. And they like it that way. And they will bite and claw against any brother or sister in Christ who tries to bring them out of the darkness.

Sometimes the fights are doctrinal in nature. Paul raised the issue of the Lord's Supper with the Corinthians, knowing it would create a stir between those who had respect for his apostolic mandates and those who did not (1 Corinthians 11:17-22).

Often the fights are personal. One party (or, usually, both) are more concerned with personal victories or slights than with the greater good of the body. Such fights can and should be moderated by concerned souls of mutual respect who can bring all parties back into peaceful harmony (Philippians 4:2-3).

Assessing blame for who started the fight is an exercise in futility. The devil started it; which of two warring brethren threw the first punch is irrelevant. The only concern should be confirming a mutual desire to be in fellowship with the Lord, then cooperation in finding where that fellowship is to be found, then patience in working through the differences in application.

Realize also, the fight may be entirely in our own head. Love "bears all things, believes all things, hopes all things, endures all things" (1 Corinthians 13:7). There is no need to assume a worst-case scenario—particularly when the one we are imagining ill of is a brother or sister in Christ.

What fights are you most accustomed to seeing among brethren? What could have been done beforehand to avoid them? _____

_____

_____

_____

Be Strong and Courageous!

1. Be strong and cou - ra - geous, you hosts of the Lord!
2. Be strong and cou - ra - geous! Through God you will win,
3. Be strong and cou - ra - geous! Con - sid - er His law;

Rise up for the bat - tle, and gird on your swords.
Though great be the ar - mies of er - ror and sin.
Re - gard it with rev - 'rence; per - form it with awe.

The land of His prom - ise is yours now by right;
Your Cap - tain will lead you to con - quer the land;
Be care - ful to fol - low all God has de - creed,

Take all He has giv - en; go forth to the fight!
His arm can - not fail you, and they can - not stand.
For then He will bless you, and you will suc - ceed.

CHORUS

Be strong and cou - ra - geous, and con - quer the foe!

The Lord God is with you wher - ev - er you go!

CODA (after last stanza)

Be strong and cou - ra - geous! Be strong and cou - ra - geous!

rit. *ff*

Be strong and cou - ra - geous!

Words: Matthew W. Bassford
Music: Glenda B. Schales
© 2001 Glenda B. Schales

Eb - 3 - DO

How strongly should we fight for our firmly held Bible opinions?_____

_____

_____

About the hymn

Glenda Barnhart Schales is a public school music teacher in the Houston, Texas, area. She has acquired a reputation as one of the finest hymnists among our brethren today. She has written music and lyrics for dozens of hymns, including some of the most popular hymns in usage today. Many of her hymns were first printed and sung regularly at the Kleinwood Church of Christ, her home congregation which also plays host to an annual singing. *Through the Bible With Songs* is a collection of 66 songs she wrote, covering every book of the Bible. A collection of 27 of her hymns, *My Father's Voice*, was recorded by the 2003 Florida College Alumni Chorus.

GLENDA BARNHART SCHALES

Her website, www.glendaschales.com, lists more than 60 hymns she makes available for individual and congregational use, as well as other singing-related materials. Perhaps the first one of her hymns to acquire a following was "The Blessed Life," a hymn based on the Beatitudes that was included in *Hymns for Worship (Revised)*. Other favorites of hers include "For You Have Promised," "Healing in its Wings," "Be Still," "You Are My Strength," and "Magnify, O Magnify." She also contributed music for hymns such as "I Will Wake the Dawn with Praises." Schales is on staff at the R.J. Stevens Singing School, where she teaches various classes.

Matthew Bassford was spending the summer of 2001 in the Houston area and meeting with the Kleinwood church. Ricky Shanks, who was the preacher there at the time, began a Sunday morning sermon by reading Joshua 1:1-9. The admonition for Joshua to "be strong and courageous" struck Bassford powerfully, and he immediately began conceiving the hymn. He finished it before lunch that same day in Schales' spare bedroom. The hymn caught on quickly, being included in *Sing to the Lord!* the next year, and later in *Hymns for Worship (Supplement)*. It was also featured on the first set of recordings from Sumphonia, *In the Midst of the Assembly*.

What do you like or not like about this hymn? _____

_____

_____

Share with the class another newer hymn that has a similar theme. Do you think this hymn does a better or worse job of teaching us about the Christian fight than "Be Strong and Courageous"? Explain your answer. _____

_____

_____

About the lyrics

Your Captain will lead you to conquer the land;
His arm cannot fail you, and they cannot stand.

Entering Canaan is a metaphor used in countless hymns. Usually the idea of entering Canaan land or crossing over Jordan has reference to death and heaven. But Bassford's lyrics give the image a completely different and equally Biblical setting—the life that we live as Christians here on earth.

Canaan was not empty when Joshua led the people in. Effort would be necessary to claim the inheritance God had promised them, going back to the generations of Abraham, Isaac and Jacob. But however daunting the task may have seemed—facing the walls of Jericho, for instance—God would give success to those who walked in faith.

We cross over from the wilderness into the land of hope and promise when we give ourselves to Jesus Christ. The waters of Jordan can even be seen as a metaphor for baptism—God guiding us through to the other side and the new life waiting for us there. But once we arrive in the kingdom of Jesus Christ, the battle has only begun. Conflict upon conflict face us as we endeavor to claim our inheritance against the opposition we face, which, again, may seem overwhelming. But with God's help, we can rest assured of our ultimate victory.

What are some everyday things that bring the love of God to our minds?

_____

_____

Is it possible to appreciate a song for its musicality so much that we ignore the lyrics or rationalize indifferent or even unscriptural lyrics? If so, give examples of songs that strike you this way. _____

_____

_____

_____

About the music: coda

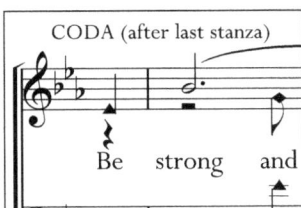

CODA (after last stanza)

Be strong and

A coda is a final section of the music, to be sung a single time at the end of the song. Occasionally music will include a *D.S. al Coda* notation. It works the same as the *D.S. al Fine*, except the music will read *Al Coda* or *To Coda* where normally a *Fine* would be found. At the *Al Coda*, instead of ending the song, the song moves ahead to the coda.

In "On Zion's Glorious Summit," an additional chant-type song called a Sanctus is added at the end. It is sung the same way a coda would be sung.

List some other songs that make use of codas. Are the songs better or worse for their inclusion? _____

_____

_____

A final admonition

Love begins with God. We can get so caught up in our expressions of love to our brethren that we forget our "first love" (Revelation 2:4). We should never allow ourselves to think that our attitude toward our brethren defines us completely. Yes, brotherly love is a proof of our discipleship to the world (John 13:35). But we became brethren because we became children of God, not the other way around. Brotherly love is an extension of our love for God.

Personal demonstrations of love for God often are private affairs—prayer, confession, thanksgiving. But they are every bit as real and important as the most public of praises. Our physical parents delight in our presence and want more than anything for us to do the same. Likewise, we must find ways to take pleasure in the presence of God.

Lesson 11

Teach Us How to
FOLLOW

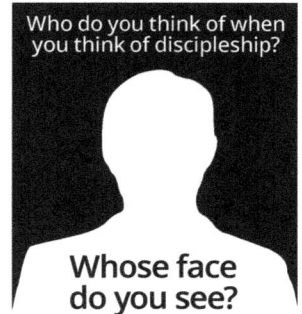

And he left everything behind, and got up and began to follow Him.
Luke 5:28

Jesus told His disciples the night He was betrayed, "I go to prepare a place for you. If I go and prepare a place for you, I will come again and receive you to Myself, that where I am, there you may be also" (John 14:2-3). He goes on to say in verse 6, "I am the way, and the truth, and the life; no one comes to the Father but through Me."

The word *disciple* literally means a follower. The first characteristic of a follower is the ability to let the leader lead. Respect for Jesus' authority will cause the true disciple to wait for His lead.

We read in 2 John 9, "Anyone who goes too far and does not abide in the teaching of Christ, does not have God; the one who abides in the teaching, he has both the Father and the Son." Only Jesus has "words of eternal life" (John 6:68), and it is not our place to decide certain "words" of His don't count, or that certain words of ours count just as much.

We cannot do all things "in the name of the Lord Jesus" (Colossians 3:17) if we are doing some things on our own authority. We have to have enough confidence in our Lord to allow Him to lead us—particularly in areas where we are inclined to trust ourselves instead. We must have a Psalm 27:14 kind of faith: "Wait for the Lord; be strong and let your heart take courage; yes, wait for the Lord."

Who is your person of discipleship? Describe the impact his or her attitude has on you and others. _____

_____

_____

Can we use song books, or song leaders, or pitching devices, or any of a dozen other recent innovations "in the name of the Lord Jesus"? _____

_____

_____

_____

About the hymn

SARAH FLOWER ADAMS

Sarah Flower Adams was an English poet, born February 22, 1805, and died at the age of 43. Easily the most celebrated work of her short career is "Nearer, My God, to Thee." She based it loosely on the story of Jacob's ladder, found in Genesis 28:11-19. Two verses omitted in many hymnals make the connection more closely:

O There let the way appear steps unto heav'n;
All that Thou sendest me in mercy giv'n;
Angels to beckon me nearer, my God, to Thee.

Then with my waking thoughts bright with Thy praise,
Out of my stony griefs Bethel I'll raise;
So by my woes to be nearer, my God, to Thee.

Adams' lyrics have been paired with a wide variety of tunes, beginning with one written by her sister. Outside of the United Kingdom, where tunes by John Bacchus Dykes and Arthur Sullivan (of the Gilbert and Sullivan musicals) are favored, the overwhelming choice is "Bethany," by Lowell Mason.

LOWELL MASON

Mason, called the father of American music education as well as the father of American church music, is largely responsible for introducing music into American public schools. Early in life, while working as a banker, he developed the habit of writing hymns and setting them to classical tunes. The collection was published as *The Handel and Haydn Society's Collection of Church Music*—anonymously, at Mason's request. An instant sensation, it encouraged Mason to leave the business world to promote vocal music in general, and sacred music in particular.

Mason's early career focused on European musical stylings for churches that emphasized the soprano line and organ accompaniment to the detriment of other parts. He had a change of heart later in life; as the musical director for Fifth Avenue Presbyterian Church in New York City, he led the effort to move American churches away from professional choirs and toward congregational singing. Although he wrote lyrics, he is far more famous for his compositions, including those for the hymns "My Faith Looks Up to Thee" and "When I Survey the Wondrous Cross."

Few songs of any genre have so much of a connection to American history as "Nearer, My God, to Thee." The Confederate army band played the song for the survivors of the tragic "Pickett's Charge" during their retreat at the Battle of Gettysburg. President William McKinley, dying of an assassin's bullet, spoke the first few lines of this, his favorite hymn, before dying; bands across the country played the song in his honor after a national five-minute period of silence. It was played at the burial of another assassinated president,

Nearer, My God, to Thee

1. Near - er, my God, to Thee, Near - er to Thee!
2. Though like the wan - der - er, The sun gone down,
3. There let the way ap - pear, Steps un - to Heav'n;
4. Then, with my wak - ing thoughts Bright with Thy praise,
5. Or, if on joy - ful wing Cleav - ing the sky,

E'en though it be a cross That rais - eth me,
Dark - ness be o - ver me, My rest a stone.
All that Thou send - est me, In mer - cy giv'n;
Out of my ston - y griefs Beth - el I'll raise;
Sun, moon, and stars for - got, Up - ward I'll fly,

Still all my song shall be, Near - er, my God, to Thee.
Yet in my dreams I'd be Near - er, my God to Thee.
An - gels to beck - on me Near - er, my God, to Thee.
So by my woes to be Near - er, my God, to Thee.
Still all my song shall be, Near - er, my God, to Thee.

Near - er, my God, to Thee, Near - er to Thee!

Words: Sarah Flower Adams
Music: "Bethany," Lowell Mason

G - 4 - MI

James A. Garfield, and at the funerals of presidents Warren Harding and Gerald Ford. The most famous connection is the tradition, disputed by some, that the song was played during the sinking of the *RMS Titanic* during the early morning hours of April 15, 1912.

What do you like or not like about this hymn? _____
_____
_____

Share with the class another older hymn that has a similar theme. Do you think this hymn does a better or worse job of teaching us about following God than "Nearer, My God, To Thee"? Explain your answer. _____
_____
_____

About the lyrics

Nearer, my God, to Thee, nearer to Thee;
E'en tho' it be a cross that raiseth me,
Still all my song shall be, Nearer, my God, to Thee!

The quest of every Christian is to be near to God, both in this life and in the next. Surely anything at all that would accomplish that goal is acceptable—even a cross. The New Testament describes three "crosses" that impact us as Christians, and any of them can be seen as the object of the first verse of "Nearer, My God, to Thee":

The cross of Christ. Jesus' own death on the cross provides the grace that saves through the blood that atones. Because Jesus has died on the cross, we have access to faith—and through faith, "the right to become children of God" (John 1:12). The cross is a gruesome sight, and drawing near to it may turn our stomachs. But God knew this was the only way sin could be truly forgiven. Because of that, the doleful song of the cross becomes a triumphant anthem of the saved.

Our own cross of submission. Paul writes, "I am crucified with Christ" in Galatians 3:20. The only way we can be lifted up to be with the Lord is on a cross. We give ourselves over wholly to Him, allow Him to connect us to the cross (at considerable pain and inconvenience sometimes), and then allow His grace to elevate us to heights of glory unattainable any other way. Self-glorification cannot lift us as high as heaven, nor can any personal achievement. Only by giving ourselves up entirely and accepting Him as Lord of our lives can we be made nearer to God.

The cross we bear daily. Jesus says in Luke 9:23, "If anyone wishes to come after Me, he must deny himself, and take up his cross daily and follow Me." Similarly, Paul writes in Romans 12:1, "present your bodies a living and holy sacrifice, acceptable to

God." Every day we live is intended to bring us in closer harmony and fellowship with God. Whatever form that "cross" may take on any given day is a small burden to bear, considering the blessing that results.

Which of these explanations of the "cross" do you think best describes the hymn's message, and why? Or do you have another explanation?_____

_____

_____

What practical implications for our lives are connected to being crucified with Christ and bearing our cross? _____

_____

_____

About the music: omitting stanzas

For various reasons, hymnal editors and song worship leaders may choose to omit one or more stanzas (a stanza is a verse plus its corresponding chorus, if any) of a hymn. But not every hymn lends itself to this treatment; as would be the case with watching the first and last half-hours of a film or reading the first and last chapters of a book, the meaning of a hymn can be muddled or lost entirely when it is submitted to the "highlight reel" approach.

Sarah Flower Adams' full lyric describes the yearning of a soul for God—in verse 2, for the downtrodden; in verse 3, for him in his dreams; in verse 4, for him after he wakens; in verse 5, for him in death. Some editors omit verses 3 and 4, perhaps thinking their references too obscure. Verse 5, intended to follow the thoughts of verse 4, fits in very well with verse 2 instead; the meaning is not lost in the slightest.

Song worship leaders often choose on their own to omit stanzas presented in the text. The last stanza of "Nearer, My God, to Thee," which begins with the word or, makes no sense when sung alone or with the first stanza only. The first stanza can stand alone or with the second stanza, but not with only one of any of the others. Song worship leaders should take the lyrics into serious consideration when thinking about singing only part of a hymn.

List some other hymns that can suffer through the omission of one or more stanzas. _____

_____

_____

List some hymns that have a single stanza that stands alone well—for instance, as a closing hymn. _____

_____

Lesson 11A

Teach Us How to
FOLLOW EVEN MORE

What can I do to have Biblical discipleship in my life?

Why isn't this me?

These are the ones who follow the Lamb wherever He goes.
Revelation 14:4

It does not take faith to go where you were going to go anyway; true faith is measured when Jesus asks us to go in inconvenient or even dangerous places. It's the kind of faith that led Abraham, Isaac and Jacob through the land of Canaan as wanderers—wandering that typifies our own wandering as "strangers and exiles on the earth" (Hebrews 11:13-16).

Do we have the faith to go into battle with only the 300 (Judges 7)? Following Christ will rarely look like the popular thing to do. But Jesus chose the narrow path, and He requires us to walk in it after Him (Matthew 7:13-14). The lack of support we get from the world is a testament to our discipleship, not evidence of its misguidedness.

Do we have the faith to stand in the plot of lentils while others turn and run (2 Samuel 23:11-12)? Jesus watched His hand-picked apostles turn on Him in the Garden of Gethsemane; yet He did not waver in His mission. We will be discouraged at the lack of participation we see among those who claim to be brethren. But that doesn't make it any less imperative that we follow Jesus. And it may be that our courage is exactly what others need to inspire them to follow us as we follow Him.

Do we have the faith to say, "We must obey God rather than men" (Acts 5:29)? The forces of this world, represented by the "beast coming up out of the sea" in Revelation 13:1-10, have always threatened the faithful with sanctions in this life. But Jesus was always about His Father's business (John 5:19); dealing with authorities, up to and including the cross, was part of God's plan. If it is part of God's plan for us to suffer similarly, we must have similar priorities.

Should unforeseen and unfortunate circumstances produce a lack of confidence in God? Why or why not?_____

_____

Do you think today's Christians would choose Jesus in the face of organized opposition from the government? Why or why not? _____

_____

_____

Break My Heart

Break my heart, dear Lord, tear the bar - riers down;

Show me in con - vict - ing tears the glo - ries of Your crown.

%℄ CHORUS

My heart is hard, my soul so weak, The ways of e - vil cut so deep;
heart is hard, my soul so weak, Ways of e - vil cut so deep,

Fine

I need You, Lord, to come in - side and gen-tly break my heart.
need You, Lord, to come in - side, gen-tly break my heart.

My sin is great but I can see the glo - ries set for me;

Show me, Fa - ther, where to start and gen - tly break my heart.

Words: Clint Rhodes
Music: David Fraze and Andy Spell, arr. R. J. Taylor
© 1997 Clint Rhodes, arr. © 2000 Taylor Publications

G - 4 - DO

About the hymn

Clint Rhodes is the campus minister at Fort Worth Christian School in North Richland Hills, Texas. He attended Harding University before graduating from Lubbock Christian University.

Rhodes was a high school sophomore when he wrote his first and only song. He was on a church youth trip and had been assigned the devotional talk for the evening. A great deal of time had been spent in the preceding days on the topic of brokenness and contriteness, and the theme had touched him deeply. The thoughts he was preparing for a devotional talk wound up taking the form of verse.

He was at an LCU camp two weeks later, where he ran into friends of his, David Fraze and Andy Spell, who paired music with his lyrics. They sung it extensively at camp that year, and the song quickly spread across the country. Within six months, Rhodes was hearing reports of his hymn being sung by Christians on the other side of the world. The song was included in the revised edition of *Praise Hymn* in 2001.

What do you like or not like about this hymn? _____
_____
_____

Share with the class another newer hymn that has a similar theme. Do you think this hymn does a better or worse job of teaching us about following Jesus than "Break My Heart"? Explain your answer. _____
_____
_____

About the lyrics

> *My heart is hard, my soul so weak,*
> *The ways of evil cut so deep;*
> *I need You Lord to come inside*
> *And gently break my heart.*

Countless songs have been written and sung over the years about broken hearts, and they are almost always sad songs. But Jesus breaks our hearts in a totally different way—not to destroy us, but to bring us to a mental and spiritual state where He is able to work His way with us.

As a wild horse is broken to wear the bridle and do his master's will, so also Jesus "breaks" us. The first of the Beatitudes is, "Blessed are the poor in spirit, for theirs is the kingdom of heaven" (Matthew 5:3). Being "poor in spirit" does not imply any sense of depression or lethargy; quite the opposite. Jesus robs us of our willfulness and stubbornness when we take His yoke and learn how to be "gentle and humble in heart" (Matthew 11:29). Compared to the burden we bore previously of finding our own way through life, despite our complete inability to do so (Jeremiah 10:23), the yoke He asks us to bear is indeed light.

As the song implies, the "breaking" process does not stop at conversion. "The ways of evil" continue to cut deep long after we give our hearts to Jesus. Long-ingrained habits are difficult to escape. But as Jesus was able to convict us enough to begin the process of transformation, He is also able to bring it to completion. He is "the Alpha and the Omega" (Revelation 21:6). Thankfully His gentleness continues to extend to us no matter how often or how violently we chafe at His direction. He continues to break us, and we—if we truly are followers of His—eventually cease kicking at the goads (Acts 26:14) and allow Him to break us even further than He already has.

What areas of our service do we tend to meet with the most stubbornness? What is the best approach for us to take in such circumstances?_____

_____

_____

Can a heart get so hard so as to be impermeable to the gospel? Explain your answer. _____

_____

_____

About the music: *D.S. al Fine*

break my   heart.

Dal Segno al Fine is direction for the singer or musician to return to the *segno* to resume the song without a break unless specifically indicated in the music. This time through the music, though, the song ends where the *Fine* is found.

Often the final measure of the score is incomplete, as with "Break My Heart"—that is, not all four beats (since the song is in 4/4 time) are represented. The remaining notes are found at the beginning of the song in the "pick-up measure." When a song features a *D.S. al Fine*, the sign will be in the middle of a measure, essentially creating another pick-up.

A similar notation, *D.C. al Fine*, is also common. *Capo* refers to the top, or beginning, of the music. Instead of looking for the *segno*, go directly to the beginning of the score;

then proceed to the *Fine* as with the *D.S.* Occasionally a simple *D.S.* is notated; in such cases, in the absence of a *Fine*, the song ends at the end of the score as usual.

List some songs that employ *D.S.* or *D.C.* notation. _____

_____

_____

Some songs, like "Tell Me the Story of Jesus," use a D.C. for the chorus of a song. List some other examples. _____

_____

_____

A final admonition

When Jesus spoke to Simon and Andrew in Mark 1:16-18, saying, "Follow Me," they did not ask where Jesus was taking them. They did not ask how long of a commitment He required, nor what might be expected of them. They left their life "immediately" to follow Him.

That is the heart of a disciple. Certainly there were time when discipleship was not what they expected. But at no point, right up to the hour Peter denied the Lord in the high priest's courtyard, do we have any indication they doubted their calling. And even that remarkable setback was overcome when Peter found his way back to the Lord again.

Discipleship is about trusting that Jesus' way is best for us and going in that way without fear or hesitation. To balk in the face of His commands and example is to say He is unworthy of being our Master, that we know better than He does. That is the attitude of a doubter, not a follower.

Lesson 12

Teach Us How to
TEACH

Teaching them to observe all that I commanded you.
Matthew 28:20

Who do you think of when
you think of teaching?

**Whose face
do you see?**

Paul told his young protégé in 2 Timothy 2:2, "The things which you have heard from me in the presence of many witnesses, entrust these to faithful men who will be able to teach others also." The willingness of Timothy and men and women like him to do exactly that, by the grace of God, is exactly why we are able to stand before God as His children today.

For Timothy, it began not with a gospel preacher but with his mother and grandmother (2 Timothy 1:5). For Apollos it began, or at least was properly redirected, by a couple of tentmakers (Acts 18:26). And for the jailer in Philippi, it appears to have begun with two singers (Acts 16:25-30).

Only the gospel is "the power of God for salvation" (Romans 1:16). But the gospel is delivered in many ways, and "teaching and admonishing one another with psalms and hymns and spiritual songs" (Colossians 3:16) may be one of the most effective. Not only is the truth delivered, but it is delivered in a memorable way and a way that demonstrates the emotional effect it has had on the singer.

Of course, it is not the gospel if it does not come from the Bible. The words of a songwriter should be measured by the word as much as the words of a teacher or preacher—even more, perhaps, since singing along implies our support of the song's message. Yes, the poetic aspect of our singing lends itself to figurative language in the same way that the poetry of the Bible does. (Try applying Psalm 91 literally sometimes!) But even poetry is an expression of truth, though not necessarily a literal one. Exaggeration, for instance, may make a story easier to understand. It can, however, get in the way. A cleverly told lie is still a lie.

Who is your person of teaching? Describe the impact his or her attitude has on you and others. _____

_____

How would you define "poetic license," and when does it become an excuse for singing words that simply are not Biblical?_____

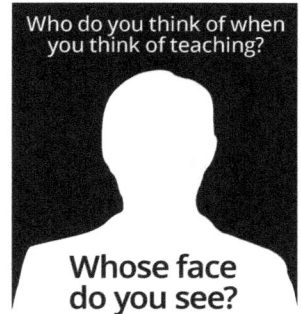

_____

_____

About the hymn

Philip Bliss was born to poverty in rural western Pennsylvania in 1838. He left home at the age of 11 to lessen the burden on his family. He was baptized a year later, although he remembered late in life he had always had an awareness of his sin and his need for the Lord.

In the winter of 1857 he met J.G. Towner, the father of D.B. Towner (composer of such hymns as "Trust and Obey," "Grace Greater than Our Sin," and "At Calvary"). While receiving instruction at the elder Towner's singing school, he met another great musical influence, William B. Bradbury. Both men encouraged him to develop his obvious musical skills. Eventually, at the urging of D.L. Moody, he quit secular work to partner with evangelist D.W. Whittle full-time.

PHILIP BLISS

His lifelong commitment to music finally paid dividends, for him and for countless others. In 1876, Bliss published *Gospel Hymns and Sacred Songs*, which became an instant hit. He refused all royalties, which reached $60,000 almost immediately, turning them back to support D.W. Whittle's work.

Bliss died in a railway accident at Ashtabula, Ohio, on December 30, 1876, along with his wife and 90 other passengers. At the time it was the worst railroad tragedy in American history. The Blisses' bodies were never recovered.

His twelve-year career in hymn writing, blessed with little in terms of formal music training, was remarkable. His hymns include "Hallelujah! What a Savior," "Almost Persuaded," "More Holiness Give Me," "Wonderful Words of Life," and "Whosoever Will." He also wrote music for others' hymns, including "It Is Well with My Soul," "I Gave My Life for Thee," and "I Bring My Sins to Thee."

Bliss quotes a story from a sermon by Moody as the inspiration to "Let the Lower Lights Be Burning"—

On a dark, stormy, night, when the waves rolled like mountains, and not a star was to be seen, a boat, rocking and plunging, neared the Cleveland harbor. "Are you sure this is Cleveland?" asked the captain, seeing only one light from the lighthouse.

"Quite sure, sir," replied the pilot.

"Where are the lower lights?"

"Gone out, sir."

"Can you make the harbor?"

"We *must*, or perish, sir!"

Let the Lower Lights Be Burning

1. Bright - ly beams our Fa-ther's mer - cy From His light-house ev - er - more,
2. Dark the night of sin has set - tled; Loud the an - gry bil-lows roar;
3. Trim your fee - ble lamp, my broth - er; Some poor sail - or tem-pest-tossed,

But to us He gives the keep - ing Of the lights a - long the shore.
Ea - ger eyes are watch - ing, long - ing For the lights a - long the shore.
Try - ing now to make the har - bor, In the dark-ness may be lost.

CHORUS

Let the low - er lights be burn - ing! Send a gleam a - cross the wave!

Some poor faint - ing, strug - gling sea-man You may res - cue, you may save.

Words: Philip P. Bliss
Music: Philip P. Bliss

B♭ - 3 - SOL

And with a strong hand and a brave heart, the old pilot turned the wheel. But alas, in the darkness he missed the channel, and with a crash upon the rocks the boat was shivered, and many a life lost in a watery grave. Brethren, the Master will take care of the great lighthouse: *let us keep the lower lights burning!*

What do you like or not like about this hymn? _____

_____

_____

Share with the class another older hymn that has a similar theme. Do you think this hymn does a better or worse job of teaching us about teaching than "Let the Lower Lights Be Burning"? Explain your answer._____

_____

_____

About the lyrics

Brightly beams our Father's mercy
From the lighthouse evermore;
But to us He gives the keeping
Of the lights along the shore.

God's light never goes out. He shines the light of salvation through Jesus; "For God, who said, 'Light shall shine out of darkness,' is the One who has shone in our hearts to give the Light of the knowledge of the glory of God in the face of Christ" (2 Corinthians 4:6). He, like His Father, "is light, and in Him there is no darkness at all" (1 John 1:5).

Our light, on the other hand, constantly wavers. We are, as Jesus said, "the light of the world" (Matthew 5:14). We maintain our confidence in our own salvation—"if we walk in the Light as He Himself is in the Light we have fellowship with one another, and the blood of Jesus His Son cleanses us from all sin" (1 John 1:7). But our moments of weakness and inattention can hinder someone who is trying to come to Christ and assuming we are helping lead them to Him.

It is incumbent upon those who try to reflect His light to do so accurately and consistently. We are supposed to be part of the solution to mankind's sin problem; woe be to us if we are part of the problem instead.

If God is capable of providing salvation "from another place" (Esther 4:14) when we remain silent, why is it necessary for us to teach at all?_____

_____

_____

How can those who are not fulltime preachers let their lights burn? _____

_____

_____

_____

About the music: dotted notes

In 4/4 time, a quarter note gets one beat, a half note gets two, a whole note gets four, and an eighth note gets half a beat. But sometimes a songwriter wants a note to last somewhere in between. That's where dotted notes come in handy. A dot to the right of a note indicates the note should receive half again its normal value. That is, a quarter note gets a beat and a half, a half note gets three beats, and a whole note gets six (in 4/4 time).

A dotted quarter note is extended a full three times longer than the eighth note that frequently follows it. Failing to hold the note long enough results in singers transitioning to the next note at different times, creating a muddy sound. On the other hand, precise articulation can help the music come alive. "Zion's Call," for instance, takes on the quality of chimes being played in precise rhythm.

be burn - ing!

Dotted eighth notes and their corresponding sixteenth notes, as appear frequently in "Let the Lower Lights Be Burning," are even easier to blur. Singing the song precisely, though, helps make the admonition come through more powerfully as words such as "burning," "fainting," and "rescue" receive extra emphasis.

Find another song with dotted notes and beat time to the words of that song as you recite the words aloud with the group. _____

_____

_____

Lesson 12A

Teach Us How to
TEACH EVEN MORE

Reprove, rebuke, exhort, with great patience and instruction.
2 Timothy 4:2

What can I do to have
Biblical teaching in my life?

**Why isn't
this me?**

Jonah had an attitude problem. He didn't want to go to Nineveh at all. When he was practically forced to go, he still harbored hatred in his heart for his audience. And when they turned from their sins, and God said they would not die, it made Jonah want to die instead.

Jonah is not a role model for teachers.

Most of the time, rotten attitudes meet with rotten results. Of course, the individual is still accountable to God, regardless of the teacher's behavior. But like Jonah, the teacher must give account to God. And just having checked the "teaching and admonishing" box does not necessarily imply that a singer is genuinely concerned about the souls of his or her fellow man. And that, after all, is the whole point of teaching them.

Some people are not demonstrative with their feelings, especially feelings of love and joy. We all understand that. But there's a world of difference between a singer who can't manage a smile and a singer who looks like he is about to have root canal surgery.

We may convince ourselves that the enthusiasm of other parties will get the job done with regard to instruction in song. But that ignores two important facts: one, that a lack of joy in our hearts (whether during a song service or not) is a direct violation of Philippians 4:4; and two, that feeling no concern for how or if we are edifying our brethren is an indication of a lack of love for our brethren, which violates 1 John 4:23. And brotherly love, remember, is the hallmark of a Christian (John 13:35).

What should we do if we genuinely do not like to sing? _____
_____
_____

What should we do if we notice a brother or sister in Christ not singing or not appear to enjoy singing during worship services? _____
_____
_____

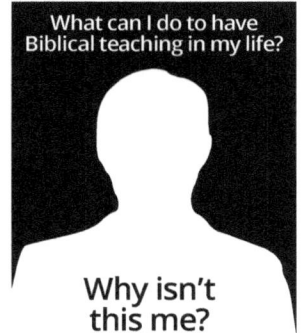

The Apples in a Seed

1. In the fruit-ful tree there is an ap-ple. Deep with-in the ap-ple, man-y seeds.
2. From the mind of God be-fore cre-a-tion, From the heart of heav-en, mer-cy's plan,
3. Do not doubt that some-one will be-lieve it, 'Though a hun-dred hear and turn a-way,

So the Fa-ther set all things in or-der, Know-ing just what ev-'ry-thing would need.
Bring-ing peace to ev-'ry tribe and na-tion, Heav-en's hope for lost and dy-ing man.
For if on-ly one heart will re-ceive it, Through the one, a thou-sand may o-bey.

You may count the seeds with-in the ap-ple, You may count the ap-ples on the tree.
God would take the bright-est Star of Heav-en, Send Him down to hang up-on a tree.
It may be a gen-tle-man of nine-ty; It may be a child of on-ly ten.

You may count the trees with-in the or-chard. Who can count the ap-ples in a seed?
Tell the world that Je-sus is re-demp-tion. Say He came to par-don you and me.
Sow the pre-cious seed for the Al-might-y. You can watch it mul-ti-ply a-gain!

CHORUS

Who can say how much the fruit will grow?
Who can count the ap-ples in a seed? Who can say how far the Word will go?
Who can say how far the Word will go?

Who can know the har-vest of to-mor-row? Who can count the ap-ples in a seed?

Words: Anne Stevens
Music: Anne Stevens
© 1999 Anne Stevens

D - 4 - DO

About the hymn

ANNE FINLEY STEVENS

Anne Finley Stevens is the daughter of longtime gospel preacher Ernest Finley and the wife of another preacher, Jimmy Stevens, currently preaching in west Texas. She has written numerous other hymns, including "Lift Up Your Voice" and "Look Up With Me!" She also wrote the music to Linda King's hymn, "Father, Love Me." All of these hymns are included in *Hymns for Worship (Supplement)*. Many more of her hymns are available at songsofthechurch.org.

The inspiration for "The Apples in a Seed" came from an article by Dennis Gulledge, originally printed in the bulletin of the Jamestown (Indiana) Church of Christ and then reprinted in Guardian of Truth in 1996. James A. Harding had preached a gospel meeting in Clark County, Kentucky, in 1877. An elder there was not pleased with the results; "Only little Jimmy Shepherd was baptized." James Shepherd went on to preach the gospel all over the world. He served as office editor for the *Gospel Advocate*. His *Handbook on Baptism* (1894) was called by James McGarvey "the best and most comprehensive work of its kind in existence." He finally passed away in 1948, having preached the gospel for six decades on at least three continents. A single "seed" had become the tool God used to accomplish tremendous things.

Gulledge summarizes his point:

> It is when we can "count the seeds in an apple" that we think the greatest amount of work is done. But the good accomplished for the cause of Christ by men and women of average existence are "the apples in the seed" that we are rarely possessed with the patience to count.

What do you like or not like about this hymn? _____

_____

_____

Share with the class another newer hymn that has a similar theme. Do you think this hymn does a better or worse job of teaching us about teaching than "The Apples In A Seed"? Explain your answer. _____

_____

_____

About the lyrics

Who can count the apples in a seed?
Who can say how much the fruit will grow?
Who can know the harvest of tomorrow?
Who can count the apples in a seed?

We always want to see results for the things we do. But results do not always appear in the short term, or even within our field of vision at all. That does not mean the results have not or will not come. It certainly doesn't mean we are wasting our time if the fields in which we labor do not seem fertile.

Paul said, "For Christ did not send me to baptize, but to preach the gospel" (1 Corinthians 1:17). His point was not that baptism wasn't important; he specifically preached, and practiced, otherwise (Acts 22:16, Romans 6:4, Galatians 3:27, etc.). He meant that he was not trying to accumulate statistics; he was merely doing the work of God as he had opportunity. "So then neither the one who plants nor the one who waters is anything, but God who causes the growth" (1 Corinthians 3:7).

When we think of visible results being the only measuring stick for our efforts, we run the risk of thinking we are somehow vital to the process—as though the gospel would not be spread without us!

Our job is to sow the seed. As Paul says in 1 Corinthians 15:58, "Therefore, my beloved brethren, be steadfast, immovable, always abounding in the work of the Lord, knowing that your toil is not in vain in the Lord." We may not live to see the full results of our effort; in fact, we certainly will not. But if God is glorified in the end, that is all that matters.

Name a preacher from the Bible who thought his efforts were for naught. Was he right?_____

_____

_____

What would happen if we knew ahead of time which fields were likely to be productive and which fields were not? _____

_____

_____

About the music: altering the pitch

Hymn composers choose a key for their works so as to maximize their musicality. Typically that means making them as easy to sing as possible. Sometimes, particularly with compositions not specifically written for congregational singing, the key is not ideal. Other times particular congregations may have strengths or weaknesses in particular singing parts; that may make it advisable to adjust the key.

The assumption should always be that the designated key is the proper one. If the song worship leader thinks the song is too high or too low, either for the group or for himself, the easiest approach is always to pick a different song. The most frequently used reason for re-pitching a song is that the leader has trouble reaching the highest note in the melody line. Realize, though, lowering the melody lowers all the other parts as well; the basses and altos can have real difficulty singing their parts if the song is pitched too low.

It is reasonable to assume the sopranos can reach a high E (the highest "space" in the treble clef staff) and that the basses can reach a low E (the lowest "line" in the bass clef staff). If re-pitching a song allows those parts to stay within the "safe range," the song likely will be easy enough for the entire group to sing at that new, adjusted pitch. This guideline will vary greatly, of course, depending on the range of the singers involved.

Sing a verse of "The Apples In A Seed" at the proper pitch, then another a tone low. Which do you prefer? _____

_____

_____

Find a song with an exceptionally high soprano line. Discuss whether pitching it lower would help it be more easy to sing. _____

_____

_____

A final admonition

Romans 6:12 is a command. Philippians 2:3 is a command. Ephesians 5:1 is a command. We may not always be the greatest at abiding by them, but as believers in inspiration and confident in the Spirit's ability to guide us into "all the truth" (John 16:13), we at least acknowledge the responsibility that is ours to try to submit. And when we fail, we apologize, make amends, and commit to do better the next time.

Ephesians 5:18-19 is a command. Colossians 3:16 is a command. What makes them any different than the others?

I am aware that some share less aptitude and/or enthusiasm for singing than others. I am also aware that aptitude and enthusiasm are not indicated in Paul's mandates in these passages—only effort and attitude. And effort and attitude are elements that can be supplied by the weakest of singers.

We cannot "speak to one another" with closed mouth. One cannot "teach and admonish" his or her brother in muttered tones inaudible even to one sitting on the same pew. (Of course, that's precisely why mutterers mutter, isn't it? So no one can hear?) Are we really so fearful of judgment from our brethren over our singing ability that we are willing to ignore the command of God?

In any society, including the church, there are givers and there are takers. Which are you during the song service?

Afterword
Remembering R.J. Stevens

He taught us how to worship.

That line, repeated often by his dear friend and frequent co-worker Dee Bowman, perhaps encapsulates best the debt owed by brothers and sisters in Christ to one of the greatest men I was ever privileged to meet.

R.J. STEVENS

Not "how to *sing*," mind you—how to *worship*. Of course, Brother Stevens did yeoman work with regard to the former. But learning how to sing is much like learning how to talk; it does little good in our service to God until we learn how to do it in such a way as to bring glory to Him. And that has little to do with technique and tonality, much like a skillful and effective sermon is far more dependent on Bible study and love for the audience than on rhetoric and grammar.

Brother Stevens taught us how to *worship*. He encouraged us all, from the professional musician to the tone-deaf amateur, to use spiritual music as a conduit to the heavenly throne. He taught us to sing with the mind and spirit first—an attitude of reverence first, then humility, thanksgiving, repentance, confidence and joy.

Most of us who knew him personally came to know him because of the singings he conducted and helped conduct around the country. Whether before a handful of worshipers in his home of Kemp, Texas, or before thousands at larger gatherings such as the Florida College Lectures, he led worship like no other. Humility in a leader is a difficult commodity, and Brother Stevens was a lesson to all in that regard. The entire community joined hearts, minds and voices gladly and without hesitation—not because he was such a great man, but because they were all serving the same great God and that worship placed in his hands would be directed to His glory and not to any man. Least of all to Brother Stevens.

His son Tim tells the story of such a session, with hundreds in attendance, in which a song worship leader chose to lead "Days of Elijah"—a contemporary song that had been placed (one might even say shoehorned) into a four-part congregational format, very syncopated, very complicated, relatively or totally unfamiliar to most of the congregation. Predictably, the group made a hash of it. Nothing was accomplished other than one man getting to lead a song he really wanted to lead—a goal that could not be further from the mission Brother Stevens was trying to accomplish. And he turned to Tim immediately afterward and said, "That song will *never* appear in any of our books." And it has not.

The books, of course, will likely be the most durable legacy left by Brother Stevens, with the exception of his songs themselves. *Sacred Selections for the Church*, known far and wide for decades among our brethren as "the red book," had been the hymnal of record for most churches of Christ since its initial publication in 1956. But it was woefully short on hymns of praise, rife with over-correction, and absent any modern offerings save (in later editions) "Our God, He Is Alive" and perhaps a small handful of others. *Songs of the Church*, which debuted in 1971, was inextricably connected in the minds of many churches to the liberal movement. A new hymnal was needed, one that would preserve the best of the old and give exposure to the best of the new. Thus *Hymns for Worship* was born in 1986, and tens of thousands of them were sold immediately—literally sight unseen. Such was the confidence brethren across the country had come to place in this man. And when he and partner Dane Shepard reworked the book and published it again in a revised version, the same churches and individuals—and many more besides— came begging for more. The books clearly could have sold for much more and we would have been glad to pay, and not feel the slightest bit less of the publishers; but he and Brother Shepard were determined to keep the books as close to cost as possible to be a blessing to as many as possible. At the time of this writing, *Hymns for Worship* is in its 17th printing and remains in pew racks across the country and the world.

The publication of *Hymns for Worship* sparked a revival in hymn writing among brethren. Suddenly dissatisfied with the offerings of denominational writers after singing the works of Brother Stevens, Brother Shepard and other writers featured in *HFW*, brethren began seeking out opportunities to learn how to put their commitment to God and to one another in song form. Here again, R.J. Stevens came to the rescue. The R.J. Stevens Singing School brought Christians from all over to (of all places) Wilburton, Oklahoma, to learn at the feet of the master and other accomplished teachers. Here Christians learned not just the mechanics of spiritual music but also the proper use of it. People who were music majors in college joined with people who didn't know whether they were sopranos or basses in a common goal—the improvement of our worship to God. Singing, now receiving the attention it deserved, became a feature of worship rather than simply what we do before and after the sermon. College students, teens, retired couples and entire families looked forward to driving four or five hours, or even more, for the opportunity to sing with the saints— especially when they heard that R.J. Stevens would be helping conduct the worship.

The increased focus on singing around the brotherhood sparked a trend toward even newer hymns—some by brethren, some not; some of great worth, some not. Churches began to supplement their hymn repertoire with newer offerings, sometimes with limited access to hymns, sometimes using questionable or outright illegal tactics. Again, R.J. Stevens did the work only he could do, putting together *Hymns for Worship (Supplement)*. New hymns, arrangements of popular camp songs, and the best of "contemporary Christian music" were put together in an attractive and edifying addition to the previous volume.

As an added bonus, Christians like never before were given the opportunity to see their own songs in print. They now had the confidence that their work would bear fruit for years to come in places they would never even visit. Before long brethren all over were singing songs by Glenda Schales, Charlotte Couchman, Craig Roberts, Richard Morrison, and a host of other extraordinarily talented poets and musicians who likely would never have had their voices heard were it not for the service and commitment of one man—the one that, to a person, they all identify as absolutely instrumental in their own work. Matt Bassford, one of the most skillful and popular of the new generation, says, "I think it's fair to say that the current proliferation of hymnists within the brotherhood has more to do with R.J. than with any other single person."

Ripples in the pond. Stevens begets Schales. Schales begets Bassford. Bassford begets another writer—perhaps in Illinois, perhaps in Ireland, perhaps in India—who will keep alive the legacy of reverential, scriptural and emotional worship in song that did not by any means begin with R.J. Stevens but that was perpetuated by him like it was by no other.

And yet R.J. Stevens went to his grave believing his contributions to the work of the Lord paled in comparison to that of gospel preachers—a strange position to take for one who was himself a skilled and beloved proclaimer of the gospel for decades. After leading singing at a gospel meeting or lecture program, he always yielded the pulpit to one who, in his mind, was doing the lion's share of the work, the work that would truly endure in the hearts and minds of those present.

With all due respect to my dear departed mentor, he was just plain wrong about that.

I have listened to recordings of sermons at such events extensively, to the point where I could practically quote the lessons from Robert Jackson, Paul Earnhart, Colly Caldwell, and many others. Yet I have received every bit as much encouragement and instruction, if not more, from singing "Immortally Arrayed," "In The Glory Of His Cross," or "We Thank Thee, Our Father"—perhaps in the congregation of God's people, perhaps just by myself in the car or the office. And it may well be that the great-grandchildren of well-respected preachers such as James Cope, Huey Hartsell and Dee Bowman may see their ancestors more remembered for "King Most High," "Thank You, Lord, for Homes," and "He'll Go With Me" than for any half-hour or hour those great men ever spent in the pulpit. And they will have R.J. Stevens to thank for that.

I can say without fear of successful contradiction that no one in my lifetime has done more good in the cause of Christ and of His people than R.J. Stevens. No preacher, no writer, no publisher, no professor. What is more, I believe, though the world and the church last a thousand years, there will never again rise up a generation that knew not R.J. Stevens. And that cannot be said of any preacher, writer, publisher or professor.

I hope, when David and Asaph yield the lectern in front of the greatest chorus of all, R.J. Stevens is given a turn.

www.ingramcontent.com/pod-product-compliance
Lightning Source LLC
LaVergne TN
LVHW061327060426
835511LV00012B/1899

* 9 7 8 1 9 4 1 4 2 2 0 6 9 *